GAMEDAY GOURMET

GAMEDAY GOURMET

MORE THAN 80 ALL-AMERICAN TAILGATE RECIPES

PABLEAUX JOHNSON

ESPN BOOKS

ISBN-13: 978-1-933060-15-6

ISBN-10: 1-933060-15-8

ESPN books are available for special promotions and
premiums. For details contact Michael Rentas, Assistant
Director, Inventory Operations, Hyperion,
77 West 66th Street, 11th floor, New York, New York 10023,
or call 212-456-0133.

Cover Design: Henry Lee
Cover Illustration: Bill Geller
Book Design: BlissDesign.com
Inside Illustrations: Christian Sean Rogers

FIRST EDITION
10 9 8 7 6 5 4 3 2 1

To Joe Blanco

who taught us to play
the whole game

CONTENTS

CHAPTER 3

CRUNCH TIME
Dips and Starters 43

CHAPTER 4

WHISTLE WETTERS
All-Weather Liquid Refreshments 59

CHAPTER 5

FIRE DRILL
Grilling and the Essence of Barbecue 75

CHAPTER 6

CHAPTER 7

CHAPTER 8

IT ISN'T EASY BEING GREEN
Vegetables and Salads

CHAPTER 9

RULES OF THE SOUTH BEND DIET

I fell in love with tailgating back in the 1970s in South Bend, Indiana, years before I played football for Notre Dame. My older brother, Bob, played there before I did, and when I was 12 years old, the whole Golic family would drive down from Chicago to watch his games. We'd always tailgate. Nothing fancy. We'd set up a little charcoal grill, fire it up, and toss on some bratwurst. Brats were huge at Notre Dame. Still are. To this day, I don't think a tailgate is complete without plenty of brats.

Later, as a player, I envied tailgating fans. When the team bus pulled into a stadium, we'd smell all the good cooking smells and see the people eating and drinking and having a blast, and I'd think, "I'm about to beat the crap out of my body, and these people are having an amazing party with great food!"

Home games were the toughest. On game day, the entire campus smelled of brats. There were grills everywhere, not just in the parking lots around the stadium. Different dorms would cook burgers and dogs and even steak. Just thinking about all those aromas caught in the crisp autumn air makes my mouth water.

Tailgating's a lot more sophisticated these days. When I called college games for ESPN a few years ago, the SEC schools had some unreal tailgating scenes. I couldn't believe some of the rigs that would roll up before the game. We're talking entire kitchens set up in the parking lot. And people dressed up to chow down. They had tents and chairs and tables and nice glasses. I remember thinking, "This isn't tailgating. This is a banquet."

My colleague in the booth, Bill Curry, and I would head out to the parking lot—or to places like the Grove at Ole Miss or the Cockaboose Railroad at South Carolina—hours before game time to walk around and sample what we could. Oh, my god, was it good. And everybody shared.

BILL CURRY'S FOUR FAVORITE PLACES TO WATCH GOLIC TAILGATE

1. BATON ROUGE, LOUISIANA. There's nothing like Tiger Stadium on Saturday night—anywhere. We had to pull Golic away from all the étouffée, crawfish, and peanut butter. (I am *not* making this up.)

2 ATHENS, GEORGIA. Here we happened upon a huge ice cream cone for Mike, which he enjoyed immensely, drawing a crowd with his incomparable slurping sounds. When the ice cream dropped to the pavement, I expected a tantrum. Mike calmly leaned over, scooped it up, placed it back on the cone, and ate every bite. (I'm not making this up either.)

3. BLACKSBURG, VIRGINIA. Where huge "gobbler legs" are barbecued and sold at filet mignon prices. Golic brought one into the booth and proceeded to wolf it down while standing behind Dave Barnett and me on camera. Dave's Mom made her one and only phone call regarding her son's career the following day. She said, "Dave, I'm sure you did not notice, but that Golic fellow was actually eating during the broadcast! I thought it was completely unprofessional."

4. EAST LANSING, MICHIGAN. We discovered one of those mix-in ice cream places and then fantasized about how much we were going to eat after the game. When we arrived at the little shop at 11:05 p.m., this lady was closing out the cash register. Even though the door was securely locked, Golic threw his 305 pounds against the window again and again. No response. He began to sob loudly into the glass, causing a huge breath spot on the window. At length he dropped his arms, looked around, and said, "I got snot on the window."

College football tailgating has become so big because college football games are all-weekend events. Pro games are on Sundays, and most fans have to work the next day. But for college games, you roll in early Saturday morning (or maybe even Friday night), and you don't have to rush right home after the game. With all the stuff going on at most college campuses Saturday night, you might even stay over until Sunday morning. Why not? You've got all day to sleep it off.

My perfect tailgate starts with finger food. Cold boiled shrimp with cocktail sauce? You bet! But chips and pretzels also make for a perfectly good kickoff. The idea is to have *something* for your nonbeer hand, even if it's just a carrot stick from the vegetable tray that you put out only to avoid catching heat from any, uh, dietarily correct guests.

Better still, try my taco salad. It's got sour cream and you put it on a big pan with tomatoes and cheese and lettuce. Basically, it's a huge pan of dip—sour cream, grated Monterey Jack, grated sharp cheddar, finely chopped jalapeños, chopped cherry tomatoes, shredded lettuce on top— that's a perfect topper for tortilla chips. It's really, *really* good.

Plus it's easy. And for me, "easy" and "eating" go together like mustard and brats.

When it comes to the main tailgating event, I'm a pretty basic guy. No lobster or steak or even ribs, thank you. That stuff's good, but I'm happier with a burger off the grill, a dog, or—you could see this coming a mile away—a well-done brat on a toasted bun, with hot mustard and maybe a little jolt of horseradish. (Ketchup? For dogs only, never brats.)

Dessert? Sure, but anything fancier than brownies (homemade) and chocolate chip cookies (homemade) is out of place at a tailgate.

That's about it, so now you're ready for...oh, yeah, I forgot one thing: the beer.

A keg's great, but there's always a danger you won't finish it, which would be a waste. Of course, there's an even bigger danger that you *will*

DON'T TRY THIS AT HOME (OR AWAY)
PROFESSIONAL EATING CONTEST RECORDS

Face it: You just ain't that tough. Football players—especially those moving mountains on the line of scrimmage—have been known to pack away more food than you can even look at. But even the most voracious guy on the Arkansas O-Line would have to take a backseat to the true hogs on the professional eating circuit. The slight Takeru Kobayashi might be the most famous eater in the world today, having inhaled a record 53¾ Nathan's Famous hot dogs, with buns, in just 12 minutes. Here are some other (nauseating) records, taken from *23 Ways to Reach First Base: The ESPN Uncyclopedia*, by Gary Belsky and Neil Fine:

BAKED BEANS

Don Lerman
6 pounds; 1:48

BIRTHDAY CAKE

Richard LeFevre
5 pounds; 11:26

BUTTER

Don Lerman
7 quarter-pound sticks (salted); 5:00

COW BRAINS

Takeru Kobayashi
17.7 pounds; 15:00

DOUGHNUTS

Eric Booker
49 (glazed); 8:00

HARD-BOILED EGGS

Sonya Thomas
65; 6:40

MAYONNAISE

Oleg Zhornitskiy
Four 32-ounce bowls; 8:00

MEAT PIES

Boyd Bulot
16 six-ounce pies; 10:00

PASTA

Cookie Jarvis
6.67 pounds (linguine); 10:00

SPAM

Richard LeFevre
6 pounds; 12:00

SWEET CORN

Joe LaRue
34 ears; 12:00

WATERMELON

Jim Reeves
13.22 pounds; 15:00

finish it and get wasted. So go with cans. (No bottles—they tend to break if dropped on pavement.) Look, I love beer as much as the next guy—especially with my brats. But you gotta remember why you're in a parking lot on a Saturday morning in the first place: to go to a football game. Some people (and you know who you are) get so messed up that they'll walk into the stadium, heads spinning, and be like, "Oh, my god, I've got to sit through a football game!"

My problem is that between the *Mike & Mike in the Morning* radio show and my other ESPN duties, I rarely have time to make it to a real tailgate anymore. That's an absolute bummer. But hopefully, things are about to change. I have two sons who are a couple of years away from playing college football. Once they hit campus, you can bet I'll be there on fall Saturdays. I'm a bit rusty, so I may need to spruce up my tailgating skills. I may even have to find an expert to give me some tips.

Better yet, I can just read this book.

See you in the parking lot.

Mike Golic
March 2007

THE SOUTH BEND DIET DO'S AND DON'TS

- **DO** keep it simple. Brats. Beer. Brownies. Anything else is gravy. (Including gravy.)

- **DO** bring enough to share. It's a big parking lot, remember. (That includes sharing with the enemy, provided they're willing to share with you. No brats for guys in the wrong jerseys unless I'm getting something back.)

- **DO** dress for comfort. If it's a hot day, give me shorts and a shirt. Heck, if my body were good enough to go shirtless, I would.

- **DO** stay warm in cold weather. The key? Keeping your hands and feet warm. That means two pair of socks and wool-lined gloves. If your hands and feet are warm, you'll be in good shape.

- **DON'T** go exotic. Anything flambé could get you arrested. And whatever you do, no sushi. (My motto: never willingly eat bait. Better to go hungry.)

- **DON'T** turn your tailgate into a Mission: Impossible. That means staying away from foods that are outrageously difficult to eat.

- **DON'T** overindulge—and yes, I do mean alcohol. You'll miss too much of the game if you do. Tailgating may be an event, but the pinnacle of that event is the game.

INTRODUCTION

INTRODUCTION

From the opening kickoff to the last
play of the NCAA championship game, the college football season is a
time for celebration. A time to rekindle connections to your school (or
school of choice), a time to scream for your team, a time to obsessively
track this year's favorite players, and, of course, a time to tailgate.

Just as the college football season has its own special meaning for diehard
fans, so does the gameday feast known as the tailgate. It's a time when
the grill connects directly to the gridiron, a pregame meal that recalls
college glory days and rekindles the connection to your alma mater—
whether or not its football program has a prayer of victory on Saturday
afternoon. It's a feast decorated in your team's colors—from Michigan's
blue-and-gold to the burnt orange of the University of Texas.

Tailgate menus reflect regional flavors and the universal appeal of the
grill. Hard-traveling LSU fans don their purple-and-gold as they roast
whole pigs, stir cauldrons of savory jambalaya, and whip up frozen
daiquiris in gasoline-powered blenders. Washington Husky fans tend slabs
of flawless Pacific salmon on their grills on the decks of their boats.
And everyone at Harvard and Auburn and UCLA gathers 'round the

A GLARING (AND INTENTIONAL) OMISSION
BUFFALO WINGS AND THE PIB FACTOR

If you're the kind of person who reads tables of contents (and you might well be), you'll probably find a glaring omission in our list of cooking projects: the all-important, ever-popular, deep-fried Buffalo chicken wing.

If there's any dish that fans would consider an essential gameday food, it would be Buffalo wings—crispy, deep-fried chicken plucked straight from searing hot oil and tossed with a rich, fiery-hot sauce (melted butter or margarine and hot pepper sauce, actually). Done right, these savory little morsels scorch the fingers, the tongue, and most of your gastrointestinal tract. Served hot on a bar-food platter, they are the essence of manly football food, despite the fact that they come with celery sticks and ranch dressing (the quintessential sorority girl side dish). Wings are a natural accompaniment to a flood tide of cold beer and even make a great projectile for "accidentally" hurling toward the screen as the rival team runs back an interception for a touchdown. They're cheap, they're available in every sports bar worth its salt, and fans munch them by the metric ton and crave them whenever they think of the gridiron.

That being said, here's why you *SHOULD NOT* make them yourself:

As any former grease jockey knows, while deep-frying may be one of the simpler forms of cooking, it requires some fairly specialized equipment to do well. A deep fryer may be a fixture in every American burger joint, but few apartments or tailgate spots have the machinery necessary to maintain proper oil temperature, fire safety, and post-cooking oil disposal. (Okay, the legions of diehards who travel with the LSU Tigers always seem to bring their commercial fryers along for fish fries, but they're the exception that proves the rule.)

The *GameDay Gourmet* is at its heart a beginner's cookbook, and deep-frying, we'll argue, is at least a varsity-level culinary skill with a very high PIB Factor (PIB for Pain In the Butt). The average teenager working a deep fryer has infrastructure at his or her disposal that you don't, either at home or at the stadium—machinery, gale-force vent hood, liquid nitrogen fire extinguisher system, liability insurance, to name just a few items. His sugar daddy, the Mongo Burger Corporation, can afford these things. You probably can't.

The dishes that we chose for *GameDay Gourmet* share a common theme — a low PIB Factor. We want you to be successful the first few times out, and deep-frying just doesn't fit into that category.

It's one thing to write "heat oil to 375°F and fry wings 15 minutes until deep golden brown"— it's another thing altogether to give you the skinny on which oils fry best, the physics of proper frying technique, and most important, how to keep your four-burner electric range from bursting into a sheet of raging flame. And don't even get us started on the folks who attempt their first Cajun fried turkey with a frozen bird. (It ain't pretty. And there are lawyers who read this stuff, doncha know.)

Besides, if you try to cook wings in your house, you're setting yourself up for disappointment. Without all the aforementioned equipment, you're likely to churn out a final product that's nowhere near as good as what you get at the drive-thru wing joint that sells 'em for a buck a dozen (celery and dip included).

In other words, put your effort into dishes that you can't order from just about any bar menu. Instead, buy 'em on the way to the game and save your energy for a more distinctive signature dish.

bright orange cooker filled with spicy, molten cheese dip. (It's okay to admit it.)

Tailgating is any school's family gathering, the party before every week's big game, and a weekly feast with friends, fellow fans, and even good-natured rivals (if they're bringing the beer).

Tailgate Food Defined

Tailgating—especially the college football variety—is not the place to get fussy. Despite what the new breed of gourmet cookbooks might tell you, a tailgate is not a fancy Saturday afternoon picnic or a variation on a dinner party at your Aunt Sophie's house. A tailgate shouldn't involve high-dollar menus, sushi rolls of any sort, or mango chutney slathered on anything.

Tailgating, my friends, is the pregame feast that demands a certain amount of blue-collar respect (and school spirit out

HAIL TO THE DIEHARDS

You know the types. The folks who pull up to the designated tailgate lot the Thursday before the game in a fully customized RV or Greyhound tour bus. The party vehicle is usually set up with sleeping room for six guests, full electrical on-site bathroom facilities, satellite hookup, and a state-o'-the-art A/V setup that runs brighter than Times Square on a Saturday night. Six-foot speaker columns pump the school fight song loud enough to drown out the marching band.

These are the diehards, and they are a sight to behold.

Where do these people come from? Are they alumni trustafarians or that sleepy dude from zoology class who hit the Powerball one lucky night? How do they save up enough vacation and sick days from work to carry them through the season? Do they even have jobs?

At the parking lots surrounding Louisiana State University's Tiger Stadium, the diehards are out in force every weekend. The cooking rigs make casual tailgaters salivate—triple-grill setups with plenty of table space, commercial deep fryers pumping out fried fish and bar-quality chicken wings, box smokers running 'round the clock. Refrigerated kegs, full bars, gasoline-powered blenders. The resulting feast would make Henry VIII blush.

Diehards, we admire your dedication; we admire your means and creativity. But here's the thing: most of us just aren't able to quit our day jobs. For most fans, the tailgate is a sacred celebration—but one that doesn't include a customized tour bus painted with our team's logo.

The good news is that as you, the reader, apply your newfound cooking prowess to the tailgate classics, you might get known for your outstanding biscuit sandwiches or "best-ever Bloody Marys." And maybe, just maybe, one of those high-rolling RV people might invite you to the big game because of your culinary skills.

ONE-FIST FOODS
THE PHYSICS OF FOOTBALL FEASTS

Great football food shouldn't require a sit-down to enjoy. At any tailgate, eating is only part of the game. There's usually plenty of mixing and milling about, animated conversation, Nerf football games, and, if your car stereo's up to the challenge, grooving to the classic rock or hip-hop hits of your choice. There might be a few nylon camp chairs around, but folks are usually standing, beer in hand, animatedly anticipating the day's contest.

With table space at a premium, there's rarely the opportunity for people to sit down to an actual place setting. Standard-size picnic plates are tough to manage in this stand-up setting and remarkably easy to overload. Ever see a well-intentioned host treat his friends to tailgate sirloins? You've got either airborne beef (there is no lap leverage with plastic knives) or a trip to the emergency room (a fork in the thigh is not a pretty sight). And as the day goes by, balance definitely becomes an issue.

Successful tailgaters acknowledge this by planning their menus (or, at least, their serving style) to this mostly vertical, one-handed reality.

Say "Hello" to one-fist foods.

By tailoring your serving style to an altered "cocktail party" format, you'll be making the most of the party's strengths—and cutting down on munch-time frustration.

HERE ARE A FEW OF THE BETTER FORMATS FOR TAILGATE DISHES

FINGER FOODS
Like dips, chips, crackers, candies, olives, deviled eggs, pork ribs, Buffalo wings, turkey legs, etc. There's a reason that these classic snack foods are so popular at tailgates—you either chomp them out of hand or eat the utensil/delivery system using humanity's most primal tool. All hail the opposable thumb.

THE SANDWICH
Or any of its variations, including the taco, meat biscuit, wrap, po' boy, sausage on a bun, and so on. The sandwich is the king of one-handed dining. A savory filling wrapped in some kind of bread appears in the cuisine of just about every culture in the world for a reason. Wrap it in a paper towel and you're good to go.

THE SMALL PLATE
For salads, bean-type dishes, pies, etc. There's a tendency to think that a full meal requires a standard-size picnic plate; instead, pack up twice as many appetizer plates and encourage people to refill often. The trick is to get plates with a radius close to that of a beer can or a plastic cup. Increased stability means fewer "tossed food" mishaps.

CUP ON THE CAN
For stews, soups, chowders, gumbos, chili. Nothing quite as brilliant as introducing some steaming, hot liquid meals to an unstable tailgating experience. Bowls are great if you've got the table space, but also keep in mind the two-cup option. A Styrofoam cup's narrow base will fit neatly on top of a beer can or, with a bit of care and juggling, in a single hand alongside your tasty beverage. This allows for a steadier stand-and-eat experience. (Your burn victims, er, I mean guests, will thank you.)

the wazoo). Tailgating comes out of the potluck tradition—making it a team sport, if you will, in which every member brings along dishes that the crowd can appreciate before the teams take the field. Fussy little finger foods (the modern-day cousins of watercress sandwiches noshed at croquet tournaments) have no place at an actual college tailgate. Ditto for Brie, baby arugula, and anything placed in an individual tartlet.

What fans crave are dishes that speak to the rough-and-tumble nature of the collegiate gridiron—slabs of meat cooked over an open flame, oversize vats of gut-warming chili, crunchy snacks and creamy dips, and plenty of beer to wash it all down. Whether you're cooking racks of fall-apart pork ribs or a fire-in-the-belly beef stew, it's all about earthy, elemental foods that you can eat before you strap on your "WE'RE #1" foam finger.

This ain't no garden party, folks. It's the feast before the battle. It's the way that fans celebrate the traditions forged in their stadiums. It's a time to gorge on foods without thinking about cholesterol, calories, or fiber content. We can eat healthy the rest of the year—gameday tailgates should be all about indulgence and celebration. From opening day until the last bowl game is done, nutrition should not be your weekend concern.

Making One for the Team

It's a rare cook who pulls off a full-bore tailgate alone—there's usually a collection of specialists who contribute a dish or more to the game. There will always be plenty of folks who fulfill their roles by bringing bags of ice or a sandwich tray from the grocery store, but if everybody took this approach, a tailgate would be about as exciting as a weekend office party.

YOUR BBQ PIT CREW
THE TAILGATING FOOD CHAIN

Like an episode of *Wild Kingdom*, there are plenty of different animals that come to feed at any outdoor tailgate. Some of them contribute to the spread; others manage to show up empty-handed damn near every week. Here's a short field guide to the different kinds of guests to help you decide where you fall on the food chain.

COOKS

SNACK SPECIALIST These guys or gals might not know a lot about football, but they usually cover the crunchy openers of a gameday feast. They'll pack the basic snack fare—chips (potato and tortilla), pretzels, peanuts, assorted munchies, and a few simple dips—so no fan ever goes hungry.

ONE-DISH WONDER The guest who makes "the best damned _____ in the world" and brings it to every game. This is a sweet spot for the beginning cook, because, as any experienced tailgater will tell you, a little gameday fame goes a long way.

THE FIREBUG Another team specialist who runs the flaming part of the feast. A pyromaniac with a Home Depot fetish, he'll bring his kettle grill, propane range, stand-alone smoker, and enough fuel to whip up a multipig luau. The week before the big game, offer to throw a few bucks toward a full tank of propane or some good charcoal. Hit him with a pair of nice long-handled tongs at the season opener and you'll always have room on his grill.

THE FANCY-FOOD FAN A deep-pocketed showoff with no sense of context. Thinks that lobster and foie gras are appropriate football fare (they're not) and that plastic plates are beneath contempt (he packs his own china instead). If conspicuous consumption is your gig, hang with these chandelier-loving fans—but the burger and beer crowd is always more fun.

SUPPORT STAFF

EQUIPMENT MANAGER The buddy who loves to call the plays and has the practical tools to back it up. Constantly on the prowl for new lightweight tables and advances in nylon chair technology—usually in appropriate team colors. Will pack his truck a few days before the game, double check the guest list, and show up the night before to cordon off the area for an away game. Keep this guy fed and happy. Away games wouldn't run as smoothly without him.

PLACE HOLDERS Any of your younger pals who don't mind camping out the night before a game to find your crew a prime spot near the stadium. Offer to feed them first and to chip in for any adult beverages that they need to keep them going through the night. Recruit younger, impressionable friends (or their kids). Worth their weight in gold, especially during conference rivalries.

THE CONSUMERS

THE CHIPMUNK Always brings a bag of store-brand tortilla chips and a jar of salsa. Opens both and then digs into the good stuff.

PUNKY BREWSTER Relives the dead-broke days of college by bringing six packs of the cheapest brew he can find. (You know, the stuff that tastes like wheat chaff and fizzy water.)

THE RANCH HAND A picky eater who tends toward the vegetarian side (often the really hot girlfriend of your most annoying college buddy). Favorite fare: celery sticks and sandblasted baby carrots from a grocery-store vegetable platter. Dips everything into ranch dressing.

THE WALKING STOMACH Shows up to every tailgate with a healthy appetite, superhuman thirst, and nothing to put on the table or in the ice chest.

THE BOOZE BOY Provides a bottle of his favorite spirit and cracks it open for the cause. (If the liquor in question is Crown Royal, he'll be wearing a vest made of purple velvet bags.) His close cousin, the Shot Gunner, might show up with tequila or a tray full of spiked Jell-O cubes. Approach with extreme caution.

As gameday gatherings have become more popular, the Tailgate Industrial Complex has overrun just about every college town in America. Supermarkets offer oversize plastic trays filled with bland sandwiches, sandblasted, bite-size vegetable pieces, and fluorescent-frosted sugar cookies that taste like sweet, sticky Styrofoam. Fast-food joints quadruple their usual chicken finger basket and pimp it to fans looking for a drive-thru solution to gameday feeding. As long as you've got 20 bucks and three minutes of spare time, you too can serve up a meal, even if it is mostly Miracle Whip.

There will be plenty of convenience foods at any given tailgate, so that's why it's important to buck that trend whenever possible. There's nothing wrong with having some prefab items, but a tailgate—whether it's a bunch of buddies clustered around the home screen or a no-holds-barred campus celebration during the annual blood-feud rivalry—just wouldn't be a tailgate without at least a few fresh-cooked dishes.

GameDay Gourmet contains a collection of dishes that reflect the different traditions that make tailgating great.

☞ **They're simple** Just about any beginning cook can follow the recipes contained in these pages with minimal fuss.

☞ **They're hearty** If you've got to sit through four frigid quarters in Wisconsin's Camp Randall Stadium or do the "sooooooWEEEEEE" hog call for three hours at Razorback Stadium in Fayetteville, Arkansas, you don't want your stomach to be rumbling at halftime.

☞ **They get better the more you practice** These dishes may be simple, but they also get better every time you make them. Truth be told, *you* get better each time you cook a dish, as you gain experience and the ability to tailor them to your own taste. Once you've nailed the basics, experiment all you want.

LEE CORSO'S
ALL-TIME TAILGATING TEAM

WHAT'S IN A NAME? Sometimes, a great deal. Tradition. Pride. Animal fats. Using only players with delicious-sounding names from every era in the history of the game, you could put together one incredible (and edible) squad.

☞ Coaches

Hayden Fry, Iowa

Thad "Pie" Vann, Southern Mississippi

Glenn "Pop" Warner, various

Frosty Westering, Pacific Lutheran

☞ Offense

QB: Bob Griese, Purdue

RB: Bubba Bean, Texas A&M

RB: Ed Marinaro, Cornell

WR: Irving Fryar, Nebraska

WR: Jerry Rice, Mississippi Valley State

OL: Nacho Albergamo, LSU

OL: Todd Burger, Penn State

OL: Art "Beef" Wheeler, Princeton

OL: Mike "Moon Pie" Wilson, Georgia

OL: Floyd "Pork Chop" Womack, Mississippi State

TE: Marv Cook, Iowa

☞ Defense

DL: Coy Bacon, Jackson State

DL: Vincent "Sweet Pea" Burns, Kentucky

DL: Joe "Turkey" Jones, Tennessee State

DL: Julius Peppers, North Carolina

DL: William "The Refrigerator" Perry, Clemson

LB: Dan Bunz, Long Beach State

LB: Jack Ham, Penn State

LB: Chris Hanburger, North Carolina

LB: Thomas "Pepper" Johnson, Ohio State

DB: Jamaal Fudge, Clemson

DB: Edward "Pig" Prather, Mississippi State

☞ Two-Way Players

End: Edgar "Eggs" Manske, Northwestern

End: Vernon "Catfish" Smith, Georgia

End: Art Weiner, North Carolina

☞ Special Teams

K: Chip Lohmiller, Minnesota

☞ Bench

QB: Marques "Biscuit" Hagans, Virginia

QB: Tony Rice, Notre Dame

RB: Dick Bass, Pacific

RB: Jeff "Sugar" Sanders, University of Memphis

FB: Roosevelt Leaks, Texas

WR: Pedro Cherry, Auburn

WR: Ken Margerum, Stanford

WR: Taco Wallace, Kansas State

OL: Vince "Bananas" Banonis, University of Detroit Mercy

OL: Chris McIntosh, Wisconsin

DB: Ken Swilling, Georgia Tech

8

How to Use This Book

GameDay Gourmet is a cookbook aimed at football fans who are tired of bringing just a six-pack to the tailgate. They might be guys with no discernable kitchen skills, or guys who know the basics of cooking, but who want to get out of the pocket and operate beyond their comfort zone.

Along with more than 80 recipes, we'll discuss basic techniques that will improve your overall cooking skills. Since most tailgating requires significant homework—cooking, chopping, prep—we cover skills and recipes that will improve your cooking both indoors (in your home kitchen) and outdoors (at the game).

GameDay Gourmet also provides instructional snippets designed to flatten your in-kitchen learning curve. Sidebars about everything including master classes, ingredient discussions, and classic dishes that make pregame tailgating a sport unto itself. "Playmakers" recommend essential gear and offer helpful tips and strategies for making the most of your cooking experience. And tips on avoiding rookie mistakes. Tailgating can be like any other game—the best teacher is experience. First-timers make mistakes, fumbles, and bone-headed moves. As a cook, you don't want these slip-ups to end up on this season's blooper reel. We'll show you what to avoid in these special sidebars.

So without further ado, let's start this show with a quick discussion of the fundamentals.

CHAPTER 1 ☛
THE FUNDAMENTALS

CHALK TALK

You've probably heard it a million times — Chris Fowler, Kirk Herbstreit, or Lee Corso yakking about how a player or team owes its success to a firm grasp of football's fundamentals. The well-executed blitz. Solid front-line blocking. Dependable short-yardage pass plays. A powerful up-the-middle running game.

The same goes for any activity — even cooking, where a grasp of kitchen fundamentals will get you ahead of the game whether you're putting together a huge spread near your alma mater's stadium or cooking up a vat of chicken gumbo for an indoor viewing of the BCS championship game.

Even though tailgating is primarily considered to be primarily an outdoor sport, the fundamentals of cooking start in the kitchen, and it's the translation of these skills from home to the gameday parking lot that makes a truly great tailgater. The key to success hinges on understanding basic concepts and gathering a small set of essential tools that will make *any* foray into the kitchen a smoother experience.

Now that may seem like a tall order for most rookie cooks raised in the microwave era. But the "cooking from scratch" process that can appear so unbearably old-school is pretty basic once you get down to it. Home cooking isn't out of reach because it's particularly difficult — it only *seems* out of reach because most cooking shows and glossy lifestyle magazines make home cooking into a fetish. And because it's always easier to speed-dial the pizza guy or fill the fridge with cryogenically frozen TV dinners (or, as they're currently called in some circles, "individually packaged microwavable entrées").

But cooking is a valuable survival skill, even in the modern world. (Because, face it, there are only so many Extra Value Meals that one person can eat). Armed with a little bit of knowledge and a few basic tools, you can start cooking for yourself and, most important on gameday, your friends who only eat home-cooked food at holidays and family reunions.

When it comes to the gameday feast, context is everything. And if you're gonna shine, you've got to see how your home kitchen and stadium spreads are connected.

FIELD OR SCREEN
TAILGATING INSIDE AND OUT

Even though tailgates started out as simple parking-lot parties, they've grown to include customized party buses, elaborate tent cities on the oak-shaded Grove at the University of Mississippi, and even fancy food spreads in front of living room high-definition plasma screens. A modern-day tailgate can take place within shouting distance of the stadium or in the comfort of your own beer-stained Barcalounger.

Outdoor Tailgating: Packing It In, Dishing It Out

Outdoor tailgates are the gold standard of tailgating and certainly the pregame party's purest form. The crowds and proximity to the playing field make any on-site party crackle with energy. Hundreds of people are decked out in team colors as they work their grills and smokers. Scalpers and last-minute spectators go trawling for tickets. Sound systems blare out school fight songs, and pregame camaraderie reaches a fever pitch. Students put the final touches on their body paint between burgers, and alumni guzzle Bloody Marys as they relive their glory days.

Cooking in your own kitchen may be damned convenient, but set up your grill in any parking lot, and it's quite literally a different ball game. (Attention, Eagle Scouts: All those years of repeating "Be prepared" and wearing those stupid shorts are about to pay off.) Advance planning is king. As with a three-day, backcountry hiking trip, you want to pack in everything you will need and pack out whatever mess you make. Ice chests replace your refrigerator. Prep space is at a premium, and if you forget the mustard or that steel ladle for the beef stew, then you've got to go all MacGyver or ask a neighbor for a gameday favor. (Next time, though, you'll surely remember the damned ladle.)

OUTDOOR ESSENTIALS

☛ Decent parking space

☛ Grill (gas or charcoal) or propane hot plate

☛ Folding tent (team colors preferred)

☛ Folding banquet/card tables (one for food, one for counter/bar space)

☛ Nylon folding chairs (preferably with cup holders)

☛ Pumpin' car stereo for blasting the school fight song or the endless pregame coverage

☛ Portable fire extinguisher

☛ Insomniac buddy with a strong back, pickup truck, and no day job

Outdoor tailgates encourage simplicity in menu and setup. (Sure, porter-house steaks *sound* like a good idea, but how are you gonna get enough leverage to cut through that bad boy with a plastic knife?) With a little bit of prep work and foresight, you will learn the skills that set the pros apart from the rookies.

Veteran tailgaters show up at the parking lot with everything they'll need and then some. After you've made one bonehead fumble in front of hungry friends ("I thought *you* were bringing the bratwurst"), you will make damned sure it doesn't happen again. That said, be sure to track those mistakes so you don't repeat them at the next game.

Indoor Tailgating: Training Camp, With Couches

Indoor tailgates—sometimes called "watch parties"—provide the host (or hosts) with distinct home-field advantages. In terms of logistics, they keep the party's activities (cooking, chilling, trash collection) centralized and more manageable. They give you the opportunity to fine-tune your chili for a few buddies without having to schlep a steaming pot out to the stadium. They also have the advantage of dependable climate control,

INDOOR ESSENTIALS

☞ TV with a decent-size screen, remote control, and mute button

☞ Table or counter space for dips and snacks

☞ Disposable plates and bowls (or one guest who likes to do the dishes)

☞ Neighbors who don't mind a few hours of high-spirited Saturday afternoon ruckus

☞ Comfortable chairs and/or a well-worn living room couch

☞ Goop-proof tarp for the couch and/or carpet if you invite Josh, that guy who always spills the salsa during field goals

G D G

readily accessible restroom facilities, and your favorite local used-car commercials during the TV timeouts.

Indoor tailgates tend to be a bit more forgiving than their on-site counterparts and are a perfect place for beginning cooks to polish their fundamentals. If you accidentally add 2 *cups* of cayenne pepper to your jambalaya instead of 2 teaspoons, you can always punt and call in the special teams (the pizza guy, the wing joint down the road) for much-needed backup.

Plus, you don't have to worry about forgetting a few crucial tools or ingredients at home. (Many is the tailgater who arrives at the game only to discover they have no ketchup for the burgers or no knife with which to take apart the beer-can chicken.)

A novice cook can also hone his cooking skills on occasions other than gameday. A good, soul-warming pot of **Lone Star Chili (p. 111)** works just as well during a Sunday NFL game, Monday Night Football, or the marathons of March Madness. Every time you make your dish and invite a few friends over, your cooking skills will increase, as will your tailgating reputation.

IN THE KITCHEN
A FEW PRESEASON MENTAL DRILLS

Aspiring tailgaters often start off pretty close to zero in terms of their kitchen skills, so a couple of quick reviews might help you to find the lay of the culinary land before you even crack open the fridge.

Know What You Like Take a few minutes and make a list of the foods you just can't live without. They might be dishes that you crave after a night of drinking (triple-garlic Sicilian pizza) or family specialties that make you feel warm and nostalgic (Aunt Rose's chicken-fried steak).

Page through the list of recipes in this book and figure out which ones trigger your drool reflex. Write down anything that makes your stomach and/or taste buds hum. Now put this list on your freezer door; if you're gonna cook, it might as well have a powerful personal payoff.

Know What You Got Take a quick tour of your kitchen. Rustle around in your cabinets, and see what tools you've got to work with. That aluminum frying pan your mom gave you when you moved into the dorms is looking kind of rough. Is that thing with the melted handle a spatula or a slotted spoon? Does this big pot hold 3 or 5 quarts? May as well also check the ingredients stashed away in your cupboards and fridge. (Beer, check. Ketchup, check. Hot sauce and spaghetti, check.) If you're missing a common tool, it'll be pretty obvious once you've got a mental inventory of your culinary playing field.

Know What You Know Too often, beginning cooks take an all-or-nothing approach in the kitchen. They feel that either they should be able to suit up instantly as a "gourmet" or they'll be consigned to the bench forever. The truth is that everyone's got *some* exposure to cooking. If you spent weekends watching your dad burn hot dogs on the backyard grill, that counts. If you worked a crappy fast-food job your junior year in high school, try to remember your griddle skills. Are you the guy that knows how to cook a T-bone to perfectly seared, just-this-side-of-mooing perfection? In the tailgating world, that, my friend, is a highly desirable talent.

PRACTICE, PRACTICE, PRACTICE

Now that you've got a pretty good idea of your kitchen situation, it's time to tell you the same thing that every Pop Warner coach tells every kid who ever straps on pads: If it's gonna work on gameday, it's got to work in practice.

And that makes perfect sense when it comes to cooking. Most people put way too much faith in recipes. They follow the steps (more or less), and if it doesn't come out of the oven or off the grill looking like a perfect cookbook photo (and it *never* does), they give up on it.

The key is to choose a tailgate dish that you really like (for example, the **Fighting Irish Beef Stew, p. 116**), and make it five times in a row. Rack up the hash marks and give yourself the opportunity to make (and correct) as many mistakes as you can.

Yes, kids, it's like Coach always said: Practice, practice, practice.

Any recipe, including the ones in this book, works in more-or-less average cooking conditions. Browning times work on the typical stovetop, but your burners might be over- or under-powered enough to add or subtract five minutes to the process. Your oven might run 25 degrees cooler than the temperature on the dial. As any kicker knows, there's no such thing as a standard 45-yard field goal; a little wind in your face or at your back can make all the difference.

The first tries at a new recipe may feel awkward, and you may end up with a few failures. (Anyone's rookie attempt at baking bread can end up tasting like a cinder block.) If so, just feed them to your neighbor's dog and try again. The goal here isn't so much instant perfection as getting yourself accustomed to the basic process. With each passing batch, your skills will increase, as will your intuitive knowledge of the dish's subtleties (kneading pressure, simmering time, etc.).

In other words, the more you cook, the better you'll be able to compensate for the field conditions on any given Saturday.

PREP SCHOOL
THE WORK BEFORE THE WORK

Want to simplify *any* cooking situation, indoor or outdoor? Take a cue from professional cooks and do your prep work before you even turn on the stove or stoke the fire.

For any chef, the working day begins with a series of simple tasks (peeling, sharpening, cutting) that streamlines the cooking process. Every restaurant kitchen is buzzing with activity hours before the first blue plate is served. Line cooks prep their dishes by preparing all the necessary ingredients beforehand, so that in the heat of a busy session, the cook doesn't have to stop to mince garlic or slice lemons in mid-sizzle. They can keep focused on the task at hand: *cooking*.

Anybody who cooks can benefit from this "cut before you cook" wisdom, primarily because it increases one's kitchen comfort level.

ROOKIE MISTAKE

TABLE ENCROACHMENT: PROTECTING THE COOK'S ZONE

The big difference between indoor and outdoor tailgates—besides four walls and a ceiling, of course—is easy access to table and counter space. It's easy to take a roomy Formica counter at a home watch party for granted, until you don't have it at your disposal. Empty plates build up, there's no place to do last-minute prep work, unexpected guests bring big bowls of their Aunt Minnie's famous bourbon-soaked banana pudding ... You get the picture.

Rookies bring a card table to the stadium; veterans pack lightweight plastic banquet tables. (If you tailgate more than twice a year, consider investing in one of these babies. Or split the cost with one of your tribe—preferably the guy with the pickup truck.)

The next task is to protect your prep space. Measure off one-quarter to one-third of the table's length and mark it with a strip of duct tape. Designate that area

as "the cook's workspace"—for cutting boards, grill-bound platters, and other necessary items. Holding that line will make your on-site cooking a *lot* easier. (Besides, what's more decorative than duct tape? Bob Vila would be proud.)

Too many times, novices will try to multitask when they're cooking. After all, why can't you melt butter in a skillet while chopping onions and thawing chicken breasts in a microwave? The reason is this: Each of those simple acts, when they're attempted simultaneously, gets more difficult, because (in the words of many kindergarten teachers) *you aren't focusing.* Performing these three elementary acts at one time splits your focus, increases your anxiety, and will make you crazy in pretty short order.

And because you'll probably miss a cue and burn the butter or accidentally nick your index finger, you'll dramatically increase your chances of screwing up and feeling like a failure. Even if your dish seems uncomplicated, you might as well be juggling a spinning saw, three rabid cats, and a smoking branding iron. Here are a few basic prep steps to help you keep your cool, and your fingers intact:

Layout Take a few minutes to gather the ingredients, pots, tools, and spices that you'll need for your dish. If you don't have tons of counter space, gather the all necessary items from the fridge, tool drawer, and spice rack. Make sure you check your recipe (if you're using one) and *look directly* at the components of your dish. That way, even if you get a bit ahead of yourself and have to scramble, you'll think "chili powder" and have a image in mind before you even reach for the ingredient. Layout also reduces the "frantic search" reflex so common to unseasoned cooks. If you take a look at everything, you'll have significantly fewer "AAAAAAAA!" experiences.

Plattering Once you've gathered the ingredients, take out a big chopping board and do all your cutting and measuring work. Now this will seem boring as hell. What you want to do is get right down to the action, don't you? ("Give me fire! Bring on the boiling oil!") But the simple act of chopping beforehand will free up your mind once you do get to the cooking.

As you prep with each recipe line item ("One medium onion, minced. Check. Two bell peppers, seeded and sliced into thin rings. Check.") transfer them from the chopping board to a large plate. If you're feeling really thorough, measure out the required spices onto a little plate as well.

Depending on the complexity of the dish, you may spend 10 to 15 minutes doing this, but it will pay off when you find yourself floating along smoothly, as the TV chefs do, instead of pitching a Woody Hayes-like food fit. ("What the hell did you do with my damned potholder?")

Cleanup This particular step is absolutely essential, but, to be honest, we're not big clean-as-you-go people here at *GameDay Gourmet*. The theory goes something like this: When you have a spare moment while cooking, walk over to the sink and wash a few bowls, knives, cutting boards, etc. Theoretically, that's absolutely fine, but you will find it infinitely more enjoyable to spend off moments shooting the breeze or arguing over the merits of the mid-major conferences. Obsessive folks *really* dig this step; otherwise, fill up the sink with your tools and dishes, and deal with them all in one swoop. Order or chaos, take your pick. We prefer chaos.

Alternate plan: A grateful dinner guest may offer to clean up. "No, no, no, no," he'll say as you start washing your blender, "you cooked!" You'd be amazed how often this happens. Just remember to put up token resistance. "If you insist ..." Hint: *Always* let them insist.

TOOL TIME
INDOOR BASICS

If it turns out that your kitchen inventory has a few gear gaps, do yourself a favor and invest in some tools that will make your cooking life a lot easier just about every time you take to the kitchen. If you've done nothing but eat takeout for decades, you could do worse than starting by getting the following items.

Pepper Mill The quickest way to give your kitchen a flavorful face-lift. Ordinary, garden-variety black pepper is the one spice guaranteed to be in every kitchen. You know it from trusty table shakers and the little square can in your apartment cupboard. It's one of our most popular seasonings, the cornerstone of the American spice rack, and usually about as tasty as sawdust. Why? Because preground pepper isn't actually pepper. It's a faded, tasteless powder resembling the real McCoy in color only. If you want real flavor, you gotta grind it yourself. Spend about thirty bucks on a decent, industrial-grade grinder, and you'll never look back.

10-Inch Chef's Knife If you've got a whole set of dull Cutco blades or an impulse-buy set of Ginsus, ditch 'em all and invest about a hundred bucks in a good chef's knife. The deep triangular shape of this blade makes it a workhorse, perfect for just about any cutting task — from dicing onions to mashing garlic to carving whole chickens. The shape of the cutting edge, a pointed tip that gracefully curves toward the knife handle, provides any cook with considerable leverage and allows for smooth, rhythmic chopping. The spear-tipped point and hefty weight make piercing and carving effortless. Chef's knives vary according to manufacturer, but the most important thing is that it feels good in your hand. Hit your local gourmet kitchenware store and test-drive a few before plunking down your hard-earned cash.

Large Cutting Board These roomy slabs of wood or white acrylic give you plenty of space for knife work. Spoil yourself with a 15 x 20-inch board and you'll actually enjoy workaday chopping sprees.

Cast-Iron Skillet If you're going to have only one frying pan, avoid aluminum and fire up the iron. Gramma used cast-iron for good reasons: It spreads the heat evenly, improves with age, and can be used to silence both sassy children and uppity in-laws. Iron has the added bonus of being cheap by modern standards—about twenty bucks for a standard 10-inch skillet—and readily available at your better hardware and sporting-goods stores. Cast-iron requires a bit of special care, but get in the habit of hand-washing these beauties and they'll last forever. (For a little bit more, Lodge Manufacturing sells preseasoned skillets and offers detailed care instructions on its website.)

PLAYMAKERS
CHILL CHESTS AND HOT BOXES

The reason so many college students limit their tailgates to cold beer and hot salsa is that their ice chest is stuffed with as many six-packs as possible, and a jar of salsa won't spoil if you open it at the game. (In many ways, tailgating is an endurance contest.) More-experienced tailgaters see their trusty insulated cooler as more than a mere brew box—it's an integral part of your on-site kitchen setup. Packed with nondiluting gel-based freezer packs, it can keep vital foods (dips, salads, garnishes, marinating meats, sandwiches, punches) safely cold for hours. Replace the ice packs with heatproof padding and your ice chest becomes a trusty hot box that helps warm foods hold their stovetop heat. (It's a gigantic, rectangular thermos, friends. If you just pack it with ice, you're missing out on half the fun.)

Tailgate vets usually build a collection of coolers for convenience and ease of packing. These are:

THE BIG ONES Save your back and select models with built-in rollers. (The best application of the wheel since the Model T.)

BEER/SODA COOLER Keeps cans and bottles appropriately cold and frosty. Gets the most open-and-shut action, so it's best to keep foodstuffs in a separate cooler.

CHILL CHEST Organizes your chilled and room-temperature delectables. Also handy for post-party dirty-dish storage.

MEAT LOCKER Bigger parties and grill gatherings might require a separate box for meats. This can help prevent cross-contamination (leakage of bacteria-laden meat juice onto other foodstuffs).

JUNIOR SIZE Bigger than a lunch pail, smaller than a bread box. For when one six-pack is enough. While I've never known that to be the case, I've heard some people enjoy portion control.

BAR ICE A one-bag cooler for the liquor and soda drinkers in the crowd. Less reach-in traffic means a cleaner drink, especially for parties with kids or your college roommate Josh. (Does that guy *ever* wash his hands?)

BRINGER OF THE BREAKFAST For the early-morning specialist—a small insulated carrier for batches of warm breakfast tacos or biscuit sandwiches.

Locking Stainless-Steel Tongs In recent years, the tongs have replaced the ubiquitous big fork in most kitchens. (Just watch the cooking shows and you'll see what we mean.) As dependable kitchen-based robot arms, they allow you to move and turn sizzling foods without danger of blisters or juice-draining fork holes.

Wooden Spoons and Spatulas Sturdy wooden spoons will hold up to just about any abuse, and they won't scrape the Teflon off nonstick cookware. They're also beautiful pieces of wood that polish up nicely with a quick rub of olive oil.

Nesting Glass Bowls Owning a whole set of these clear-glass containers — running from "holds a turkey" big to "pinch of salt" tiny — will save your sanity when you're doing your pregame prep work. Check your local cooking store for a durable Pyrex set.

TOOL TIME
OUTDOOR GAME SAVERS

It's pretty easy to tick off the things you need for a basic grill-centric tailgate (grill, ice, beer, chips), but it's the little things that will make or break your gameday festivities. Here are a few items that can make your football season Saturdays a *whole* lot easier.

Extra Ice Any veteran tailgater knows that a football party depends on fire and ice: Run out of either and the situation can get pretty tense. On that last grocery run on the way to the game, pick up a couple more bags of ice than you think you'll need to keep things cool or to keep pour-your-own cocktails chilled. Hardcore party-throwers keep a stock of plastic gel-packs for lots of cooling power without watery residue.

Disposable Roasting Pans These spacious utility players, made of heavy-duty aluminum foil, are perfect for organizing and transporting just about anything to the designated tailgate spot. And, as a bonus, once the party's done, you can crumple them up and hit the recycling dumpster from fifteen yards out. (If you've got the arm, that is . . .)

Zip-Top Plastic Food Bags Another handy way of keeping track of your pre-prepped ingredients (marinating meats, chopped vegetables, etc.).

Waterless Hand Sanitizer In the absence of running water, a true boon to the clean-hands club. Grab a few bottles at the drug store and make sure your grill tenders use it whenever they've handled raw meat — just to be safe.

Industrial-Strength Trash Bags Big, thick bags make postparty cleanup a lot easier.

THE ULTIMATE GAMEDAY SPREAD

So many foods, so little time. With a collective 39 years' worth of *College GameDay* experience, Kirk Herbstreit, Lee Corso, and Chris Fowler have sampled more tailgate menus than you're likely to dream about. Why not heed their advice?

DOs

KIRK: "Plenty of sides. There's one, I think they call 'em party potatoes. It's like potatoes and cheese and Rice Krispies and sour cream all mixed up in a casserole. Who knows what's really in there? But if there's some cheese-and-potato concoction available, I'm generally the first in line."

LEE: "You just can't beat bratwurst, especially in Wisconsin."

CHRIS: "Prime cuts of meat are a must, nicely marinated and cooked medium rare. And I will probably catch hell for this, but there's nothing wrong with a nice bottle of red wine. If you take the care to get a good steak, you might as well have the wine to go with it."

DON'Ts

KIRK: "Don't run out of anything. Folks who do this right know that abundance is key. The amount of food they prepare, you'd think they were feeding the whole stadium."

LEE: "I've seen deep-fried snake served. Not so sure about that."

CHRIS: "Anything with mayo in it that's left out in the sun needs to be avoided at all costs. And while I'm not opposed to a nice shrimp cocktail, I draw the line at sushi. Parking lots and raw fish just don't mix."

Electric Generator This clearly goes in the category of "extra points," but at a lot of schools, it's fairly common for tailgaters to rev up a gas-powered generator to add juice to their hot plates, cocktail blenders, and audio-video setups. It also helps to bring some comforts of home (and the home kitchen) to the great outdoors.

Empty Cooler Just in case. Comes in extra handy when you've got to transport a big pot of chili to the game. Pack the lidded pot securely with towels or other heat-resistant packing. Protects your car's interior (or passengers' laps) from high-velocity slosh stains. Helps you hang on to your friends.

CHAPTER 2
GET YOUR GAME FACE ON

BREAKFAST AND BAKED GOODS

CHALK TALK

Want to be hailed as a tailgate hero? Be the guy who brings the breakfast. So many times in the precious hours before kickoff, we're so focused on the savory dishes, the grill logistics, and stocking the ice chest that we forget what our mamas told us about breakfast being the most important meal of the day. Between trips to the car, we somehow skip breakfast just about every time.

This is especially true with a noon kickoff—and in preparation your buddies haven't thought much beyond burgers and beer. If you roll up to the stadium with a bag of warm **Longhorn Breakfast Tacos (p. 32)**, or bacon sandwiches made with **Hall of Fame Homemade Biscuits (p. 37)**, they'll be gone about two minutes later.

The fact is that breakfast sandwiches power the whole tailgate process. Nobody's got time to mess around during setup, so as much as you'd like to cook pancakes on the grill, it's really better to choose dishes that respect the limitations of the parking lot than try to emulate your favorite diner experience.

There are plenty of good dishes that can fill you up in the early hours of gameday. Think portable and warm, hearty, yet compact enough to eat with one hand in between tailgate chores like prepping the grill, setting up tables, and arguing with your buddies about who's the best conference linebacker of all time. You know, the important stuff. Mix in a few general-purpose baked goods and you're good to go. (And if you haven't had good corn bread to go along with your chili, like our **Iron Skillet Corn Bread on p. 36,** then you're missing one of life's great pleasures.)

PLAYMAKER
LONGHORN BREAKFAST TACOS

These easy-to-make, hearty Tex-Mex breakfast treats are the standard morning fare at the University of Texas at Austin, where the *taquerias* in the city ramp up early to feed the 50,000 students. If you know how to scramble an egg, cook bacon, and shred cheese, you can whip up a batch of these South-of-the-Border McMuffins in no time.

The process is simple: Get a dozen flour tortillas, a dozen eggs, and a half pound each of bacon, breakfast sausage, and sharp cheddar cheese. Fry up the meat products until crispy, and set aside. Shred the cheese. Warm the tortillas slightly in the oven, and gently scramble the eggs. Get out a roll of aluminum foil.

At this point, it's more about assembly than cooking. Plop a tortilla on a square of foil, load it up with a little egg and the topping of your choice. (Mix it up and make some bacon/egg, sausage/egg, egg/cheese, bacon/cheese variations. You get the idea.) Fold 'em like a fat, savory cigar, and mark the outside of each with a felt-tip Sharpie so you can identify the different varieties (especially important for your vegetarian friends). A squeeze-bottle of your favorite salsa makes a nice touch for the chili-heads in your party. Bring an insulated bag (or better yet, a small lunchbox-size cooler) of these foil-wrapped beauties to your morning tailgate and watch 'em disappear.

G D G

SERVES 12

HOGS IN A BLANKET

The lovechild of the hot biscuit and savory bleacher dog, these tasty bites make for snackable early-morning food that can be prepped the night before and baked right before you head out to the game. Plus, if your team happens to be playing the University of Arkansas, Hogs in a Blanket provide awesome taunting material (especially if you're confident of your secondary's ability with coverage).

THE INGREDIENTS

I (8-ounce) can of refrigerated crescent dinner rolls
I pound maple breakfast sausage links, cooked according to
    package directions
1/4 cup maple syrup
2 tablespoons brown mustard

THE DRILL

I. Preheat the oven to 375°F. Gently separate the dough into 4 equal rectangles. Seal the remaining perforations together with your fingertips. Cut each rectangle lengthwise into three strips.

2. Top one strip of the dough with a sausage link and roll it up. Seal the seam and place, seam-side down, on a large ungreased baking sheet. Repeat with the remaining dough strips and sausages, placing them about two inches apart on the sheet. (This dish can be made ahead of time to this point. Just cover the sheet with plastic wrap and refrigerate overnight.) Bake until the dough is puffed and golden brown, about 15 minutes.

3. Meanwhile, to make the dipping sauce, in a small bowl combine the maple syrup and the mustard. Serve the "hogs" hot with the sauce.

KEG OF NAILS BEER BATTER BREAD

MAKES 1 LOAF

Three words: easiest bread ever. Even the most bare-bones bachelor can scratch up the ingredients for this easy morning baking project. (You *do* have beer in the fridge, don't you?) Combine the dry ingredients the night before and you can have fresh-baked bread by the time the second cup of weekend coffee hits your brain. Spread liberally with butter and you've turned the staff of life into a tailgate magic trick.

THE INGREDIENTS

3 cups self-rising flour
3 tablespoons sugar
Pinch salt
1 (12-ounce) can or bottle of beer, at room temperature
2 tablespoons butter, melted

THE DRILL

1. Preheat the oven to 350°F. Grease a 9 x 5-inch loaf pan.

2. In a large bowl, combine the flour, sugar, and salt with a big spoon. Gradually add the beer, stirring constantly, until a stiff batter forms. (The batter doesn't have to be completely smooth, but most of the lumps should be beaten out of it.)

3. Pour the batter into the pan. Bake for 25 minutes, then drizzle the melted butter over the top. Return to the oven and bake until the top is golden and the bread sounds hollow when tapped on the bottom (about 20 to 25 minutes longer). Cool the loaf in the pan about 15 minutes. Remove from the pan and place on a wire rack to cool. Serve warm, or cool completely.

NO PLACE TO START A FOOD FIGHT

College rivalries come in all shapes and sizes. Lehigh-Lafayette boasts the most longevity (1884), Louisville-Cincinnati the toughest-sounding trophy (the Keg of Nails), and Florida State-Miami the most heartbreak for a generation of field goal kickers. So it takes a special kind of loathing to become one. Here are some of the *GameDay* crew's favorites.

THE ARMY-NAVY GAME, FIRST PLAYED IN 1890
ARMY VS. NAVY (NAVY LEADS THE SERIES, 51–49–7)

The pageantry, the procession, that forever-unflappable goat. Nobody this side of Roger Staubach's age remembers when the game had national championship implications, but it would be positively un-American to tune the two teams out. The day we stop watching and cheering, the terrorists will have won.

THE BIG GAME, 1892
STANFORD VS. CAL (STANFORD, 54–44–11)

Herbert Hoover was the Stanford team manager for the first Big Game; Cal fans were the first to perform "card stunts," at halftime in 1910; but what everyone remembers is the 1982 multilateral, crash-through-the-band, last-second kick-off return, known simply as "The

Play." Announcer Joe Starkey called it "the most amazing, sensational, dramatic, heart-rending, exciting, thrilling finish in the history of college football!" Which was an understatement.

THE IRON BOWL, 1893
ALABAMA VS. AUBURN (ALABAMA, 38–32–1)

The best-known (okay, most-documented) intrastate rivalry in America is notorious for dividing couples, families, and the Alabama statehouse. Says Lee Corso: "The old Iron Bowl games in Birmingham, before they went to the home-and-away format, were an incredible scene. People would camp out starting on Sunday, *six days* before the game."

THE GAME, 1897
MICHIGAN VS. OHIO STATE (MICHIGAN, 57–40–6)

"My personal favorite is Ohio State-Michigan," says Kirk Herbstreit, who played quarterback for the Buckeyes in the early '90s. "There's so much at stake year after year," he explains. "It's always freezing cold. The fans have such long memories and it's clear that they really don't like each other. At some other so-called rivalries, you might see opposing fans

mingling together with a good-natured ribbing vibe. Not at this one. No way."

THE RED RIVER RIVALRY, 1900
TEXAS VS. OKLAHOMA (TEXAS, 57–39–5)

Played in the oddly neutral site of the Cotton Bowl, this game matters so much that not one, not two, but three trophies are exchanged at game's end (one each to the winning athletic department, student government, and state governor). Says Chris Fowler: "The Texas State Fair is an incredible backdrop, and the whole scene feels like a trip back in time."

THE WORLD'S LARGEST OUTDOOR COCKTAIL PARTY, 1912
GEORGIA VS. FLORIDA (GEORGIA, 45–37–2)

Also partaking in the "Deep South's Oldest Rivalry" (against Auburn) and a "Clean, Old-Fashioned Hate" (Georgia Tech), the Bulldogs clearly have a knack for this. The pregame tailgate party is what makes this matchup stand out. The NCAA, trying to distance itself from all the boozing, asked the television networks to stop referring to the game by its famous nickname. Didn't work.

IRON SKILLET CORN BREAD

SERVES 8

SMU and TCU fans: Believe it or not, this one's not about you. Iron skillets have been common kitchen accoutrements since well before Southern Methodist and Texas Christian began battling each other on the football field. In fact, this version of that Southern staple corn bread adds a whole lot of flavor to *any* party that involves a big pot of chili. For indoor tailgates, cut the bread and serve straight from the skillet (after the iron's had a chance to cool down, of course). If you're headed out to the stadium, wrap the disk-shaped loaf in foil for easy, crumple-up cleanup.

THE INGREDIENTS

3/4 cup ✚ I tablespoon corn oil
I I/2 cups canned cream-style corn
I I/2 cups sour cream
3 large eggs, lightly beaten
I I/2 cups self-rising cornmeal mix (preferably White Lily
 or another regional brand)

THE DRILL

I. Pour one tablespoon of oil into a 10-inch cast-iron skillet. Place the skillet in the oven and preheat the oven to 425°F.

2. Combine the corn, sour cream, eggs, and the remaining 3/4 cup of oil in a large bowl. Add the cornmeal mix and stir until just blended.

3. Remove the hot skillet from the oven. Carefully pour the batter into the skillet. Place skillet in the oven again and reduce the oven temperature to 375°F. Bake until golden brown and a toothpick inserted into the center comes out clean, about 40 minutes. Serve warm, or cool completely.

MAKES ABOUT 12 BISCUITS

THE HALL OF FAME HOMEMADE BISCUIT

In most parts of the South, the biscuit reigns supreme as the breakfast bread of choice. Whether soaking up thick cream gravy or smeared with sweet strawberry preserves, a real homemade biscuit can be truly magical.

THE INGREDIENTS

2 cups self-rising, soft-wheat flour (preferably White Lily or another regional brand)

1/4 cup vegetable shortening, butter, or lard

2/3 to 3/4 cup milk or buttermilk

THE DRILL

1. Preheat the oven to 500°F. Line a large baking sheet with parchment paper.

2. Combine shortening and flour in a large bowl. With a pastry blender, fork, or your fingertips, cut in the shortening until the mixture resembles coarse crumbs. Gradually fold in enough of the milk until the mixture no longer sticks to the side of the bowl and a dough is formed.

3. Turn the dough onto a lightly-floured surface. Dust your hands lightly with flour. Fold the dough in half and press lightly. Repeat. Pick up the dough if it sticks to the surface and lightly dust with flour. Fold two or three more times, until the dough is not sticky on the outside but remains sticky inside. Lightly roll with a rolling pin or pat the dough to a 1/2-inch thickness.

4. With a floured biscuit-cutter or a three-inch round cookie-cutter, cut out biscuits (do not twist the cutter). Place the biscuits on the baking sheet (one inch apart for crisp-sided biscuits or touching for soft-sided biscuits). Bake until the tops are browned, 8 to 10 minutes. Cool on the baking sheet for at least one minute. Serve warm.

SPECIAL TEAMS

THE BISCUIT SANDWICH

Like the Longhorn Breakfast Tacos (p. 32), these versatile pillows of bready goodness are more than welcome at any early-kickoff tailgate. Whether you're starting with homemade biscuits or the quicker "dough in a tube" store-bought variety, ham, bacon, and/or sausage biscuit sandwiches can make you very, very popular during a gameday morning gathering. Split the biscuits, while still warm, with a fork, slather them with butter, and insert a couple slices of your favorite jelly or breakfast meat. Wrap each sandwich in foil and mark it with an ingredient code (B=bacon, etc.). A six pack-size, insulated cooler can hold a couple of dozen circular sandwiches, which should be plenty to solidify your tailgate credibility among a group of hungry buddies.

CARAMEL-APPLE CREAM BISCUITS

SERVES 10 TO 12

This simple fondue-like biscuit combo is proof positive that you can never have enough sticky sugar on the table at a tailgate. The underlying biscuits are simpler than their homemade Southern cousins, and the buttery caramel sauce is pretty good camouflage for sneaking fresh fruit into your gameday diet.

THE INGREDIENTS

- 2 1/2 cups self-rising soft-wheat flour (preferably White Lily or another regional brand)
- 2 tablespoons sugar
- 1 1/2 cups heavy (whipping) cream
- 2 tablespoons butter or margarine, melted

PLAYMAKER
REGIONAL STAPLES

These days, a lot of cooks don't think much about the dry stuff that goes into their baked goods—mainly because they don't actually do a lot of baking (thanks mainly to dough-in-a-tube technology). Most folks will buy a bag of all-purpose flour (some national or store brand, whatever's cheapest) and stash it in the back of their pantry. But if you're aiming to become a biscuit specialist, you'll want to pay a bit more attention to your choice of ingredients. To achieve a better—read: lighter—texture for your dough, you'll need a flour that's made of "soft wheat" (lower in protein, perfect for biscuits) instead of "hard wheat" (higher in protein, better for breads). If your grandmother's from the South and bakes kick-ass biscuits, odds are she uses a special brand of flour. White Lily is our favorite. In some regions, you can find soft wheat flours alongside the hard in the grocery store; other places, these varieties might require setting foot in the—gulp!—gourmet section, or even a trip to a specialty-foods store. Either way, the end product will be noticeably improved.

Same goes for cornmeal. The national brands may last a long time on the shelf, but the cornbread they produce may be a bit on the one-dimensional side. Read a few labels on the cornmeal bags and pick whichever one is milled closest to your hometown. And one more thing: Don't be afraid to pay a little bit more for the good stuff.

For the topping:

1 (18-ounce) tub refrigerated caramel-apple dip
2 Golden Delicious or Granny Smith apples, peeled and
    finely chopped
1/2 cup pecans, walnuts, or peanuts, toasted and finely
    chopped (optional)
2 tablespoons butter or margarine

THE DRILL

1. Preheat the oven to 450°F. Lightly coat a large baking sheet with
nonstick cooking spray.

2. In a medium bowl, combine the flour and the sugar. Add the cream
and stir until the mixture forms a ball. Turn the dough out onto a
lightly floured surface. Lightly knead the dough until pliable—roughly
three to five times—adding just enough flour to keep the dough from
sticking to your hands. Do not overwork the dough.

3. Lightly roll the dough with a rolling pin to a 1/2-inch thickness.
With a floured 1 1/2-inch round cutter, cut out the biscuits. Reroll the
scraps and cut more biscuits. Place them one inch apart on the baking
sheet and brush with the melted butter. Bake the biscuits until golden
brown, about 10 minutes. Transfer to a wire rack and cool completely.

4. Meanwhile, make the topping. In a large microwavable bowl, combine
the caramel-apple dip, apples, nuts (if using), and butter. Microwave on
"High" until the mixture is heated through, about one minute, stirring
once halfway through cooking. Serve warm with the biscuits.

ROOKIE MISTAKE

NO OVEN THERMOMETER

KITCHEN REALITY #347: Never
trust your oven's temperature
dial. Many is the inattentive
novice baker who cranked up
his hot box to 350° F, set the
timer for 15 minutes, and ended
up with smoldering slabs of
carbon or pucks of raw dough
instead of fluffy, white biscuits.

Despite what your dial tells
you, **YOUR OVEN'S HEAT LEVEL
MAY WELL BE WRONG** by 25°F
to 50°F in either direction. So
cover yourself by investing in
a ten-dollar metal thermometer that you can just leave in
your oven.

It doesn't take long to get into
the habit of double-checking
the heat, and this one, simple
act can make all the difference in baked goods being
delicious and golden brown
(the way that your gramma
intended them).

STICKY FINGERS MONKEY BREAD

SERVES 8

As much as we would *love* to start this recipe by writing "Take three medium-size baboons," we can't. Lawyers are involved. And baboons, for all their other charms, don't bake very well. Even so, this cake-shaped riff on the familiar cinnamon bun is a pull-apart Midwestern favorite that is always a hit, especially with already sticky-fingered kids. Tailgate Tip: If you've got nieces and/or nephews at the party, give them a handful, point them at their parents, and say "Go tackle Mommy and Daddy." Instant fun.

THE INGREDIENTS

3 (12-ounce) cans refrigerated biscuits
1 cup granulated sugar
2 teaspoons ground cinnamon
1/2 cup walnuts or pecans, chopped
1/2 cup raisins
1/2 cup butter
1 cup firmly packed brown sugar

THE DRILL

1. Preheat the oven to 350°F. Grease a 10 x 4-inch tube pan. (Do a Google image search if you have any question about what this might be.)

2. Combine the granulated sugar and cinnamon in a large zip-top plastic bag. Cut each biscuit into quarters. Working with six to eight pieces at a time, add the biscuits to the cinnamon-sugar mixture; seal and shake to coat. Arrange enough biscuits in the prepared pan to fill the bottom; lightly sprinkle with some of the walnuts and raisins. Repeat the process with the remaining biscuits, cinnamon-sugar mixture, walnuts, and raisins.

3. In a small saucepan, combine the brown sugar and butter; cook over medium heat until the butter melts. Increase the heat and boil for one minute. Pour over the biscuits. Bake until the top is golden and a toothpick inserted into the center comes out clean, about 35 minutes. Cool the bread in the pan, about 10 minutes. Remove from the pan and place on a serving plate to cool completely. To serve, pull the biscuits apart with your fingers.

MAKES
10 STICKY
BUNS

HAPPY VALLEY STICKY BUNS

The original version of this Penn State classic is drenched in butter and warmed on the griddle at Ye Old College Diner in State College—the late-night hangout that makes this legendary sweet treat—until the crust is all sweet, crunchy, and spicy. Ours is made for heating on the morning grill—close enough to bakery fresh for gameday purposes. If there are any left over (and that's a very big "if"), these treats morph into dessert with a little bit of added ice cream and chocolate syrup—and the grilled sticky sundae is born.

THE INGREDIENTS

1/2 cup unsalted butter, melted
1/2 cup firmly packed brown sugar
1/2 cup raisins
1 cup chopped pecans
2 tablespoons dark corn syrup
2 (1-pound, 1 1/2-ounce) cans (5-count each) refrigerated
    cinnamon rolls with icing
Butter, for serving

THE DRILL

1. Preheat the oven to 375°F. Pour 1/4 cup of the melted butter into each of two 9-inch round cake pans. Layer each with 1/4 cup of the brown sugar, 1/4 cup of the raisins, and 1/2 cup of the pecans. Drizzle the tops with one tablespoon of the corn syrup.

2. Separate each can of dough into five rolls; reserve the icing. Place five of the rolls, cinnamon-side down, over sugar-pecan mixture in each pan.

3. Bake until the rolls are a deep golden brown and the sugar mixture is bubbly, about 30 minutes. Cool in the pans about five minutes. To remove from the mold, place a plate over each pan and invert. With a rubber spatula, scrape any remaining sugar mixture from the pans and onto the buns. Drizzle the tops with the reserved icing and cool completely.

more

4. To serve at home, melt about one tablespoon butter in a large non-stick skillet or griddle over medium heat. Add the buns, in batches if necessary, and cook until heated through, two to three minutes on each side. To serve at a tailgate, pack the buns in a 13 x 9-inch foil pan with a lid. Oil a grill rack and preheat the grill. Add the buns to the grill rack and grill until heated through, one to two minutes on each side.

CLASSIC TAILGATING
STATE COLLEGE, PENNSYLVANIA

On football weekends, State College has been known to double in size, in no small part due to the traveling caravan that sets up shop outside the team's mammoth Happy Valley home. Along with the usual suspects, culinary specialties include stromboli, bacon-wrapped shrimp dunked in barbecue sauce, pickled eggs, kielbasa, and, of course, Sloppy Joes. But the ideal dessert, hands down, is ice cream from Penn State's famous creamery. Novices will tell you to order the Peachy Paterno. We recommend the Bittersweet Mint.

Chris Fowler says, "North of the Mason-Dixon line, Penn State is my favorite tailgating scene. It doesn't matter who they're playing or what their record is, folks are so excited. And it really captures that collegiate feel, with everybody bundled up for the cold and the kids playing Nerf football."

G D G

CHAPTER 3
CRUNCH TIME

DIPS AND STARTERS

CHALK TALK

Easy to make (and make ahead) dips are a great way to get your tailgate game upfield fast. Throw down a bowl of chunky guacamole or cheesy artichoke dip and it's like you just started the game clock. As the ribs sizzle on the grill or the jambalaya warms on the burner, your tailgaters will start circling, crunching a bite (or two or three) in between injury reports, point-spread predictions, and getting game faces on.

With dips, there's never any waiting, and since the serving utensil is most always edible, cleanup is only necessary for those who overestimate the chip's load capacity. (In some circles, the tailgate hasn't officially started until Uncle Louie drops a big blob of bean dip down the front of his shirt.) And these simple, make-ahead nibbles buy you a bit of time with which to finish off your bigger-ticket items on the grill or in the pot.

SEVEN-COUNT LAYERED MEXICAN DIP

SERVES
6

Essentially a pan of full-fat taco components — bean dip, sour cream, salsa — this suburbanized take on Tex-Mex cuisine has been around as long as Fritos. Our version can be prepared as is, or, for a meaty kick, layered with a pound of well-browned hamburger in place of the avocados.

Note: When it comes to serving sizes, it's all relative. We don't mean to imply that your fat Uncle Joe tips the scale — well, maybe he does, but that's not really our business, is it? — but rather, that it all depends on the amplitude of your spread. This dip, acting as your solo starter, will comfortably serve three or four people. More, obviously, in combo with other appetizers. The figures given in these recipes assume that you will have two or so starters, enough to be considered generous but not quite to the level of an overzealous booster.

THE INGREDIENTS

2 to 3 ripe avocados, mashed
2 tablespoons fresh lemon juice
1/2 teaspoon salt
1/4 teaspoon cracked black pepper
1 (8-ounce) container sour cream
1/2 cup mayonnaise, preferably Hellmann's
1 (1 1/4 ounces) package taco seasoning
2 (9-ounce) cans bean dip
1 large bunch scallions, chopped
3 tomatoes, diced
1 (6-ounce) can whole pitted black olives, drained and sliced
1 (8-ounce) package shredded cheddar cheese
1 large bag tortilla chips

THE DRILL

1. In a medium bowl, combine the avocados, lemon juice, salt, and pepper.

2. In a small bowl, combine the sour cream, mayonnaise, and taco seasoning.

3. Spread the bean dip in a 13 x 9-inch baking dish. Layer the top with the avocado and sour cream mixtures, in that order. Cover the dish with plastic wrap.

4. Line three airtight plastic containers with paper towels. Place the tomatoes, scallions, and olives in separate containers and cover.

5. Refrigerate everything overnight.

6. When ready to serve, combine the tomatoes, scallions, and olives in a medium bowl. Uncover the dip and sprinkle with the tomato mixture. Top evenly with the cheese.

7. Pass the tortilla chips.

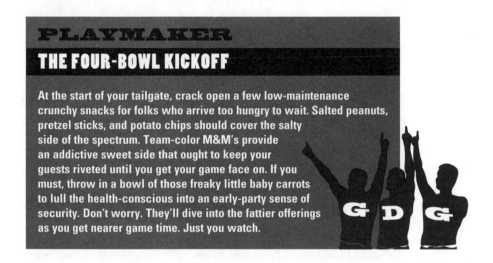

PLAYMAKER

THE FOUR-BOWL KICKOFF

At the start of your tailgate, crack open a few low-maintenance crunchy snacks for folks who arrive too hungry to wait. Salted peanuts, pretzel sticks, and potato chips should cover the salty side of the spectrum. Team-color M&M's provide an addictive sweet side that ought to keep your guests riveted until you get your game face on. If you must, throw in a bowl of those freaky little baby carrots to lull the health-conscious into an early-party sense of security. Don't worry. They'll dive into the fattier offerings as you get nearer game time. Just you watch.

BLUE DEVIL CHEESE AND BACON DIP

SERVES 6 TO 8

Easy to make and even easier to devour, this dip is a crowd-pleaser that's hugely popular at Duke tailgates and welcome anywhere that big flavors reign. Thick-sliced, peppered bacon gives the dip a distinctly porky flavor.

THE INGREDIENTS

1 (8-ounce) tub whipped cream cheese
3/4 cup crumbled Danish blue cheese
3/4 cup sour cream
2 tablespoons mayonnaise
1 teaspoon prepared horseradish
2 tablespoons minced onion
1 tablespoon Italian seasoning
Dash hot pepper sauce
6 slices peppered bacon, cooked until crisp and crumbled
Apple wedges, cut-up raw vegetables, and/or Wheat Thins

THE DRILL

1. Put the cream cheese, blue cheese, sour cream, mayonnaise, horseradish, onion, Italian seasoning, and pepper sauce in a food processor. Pulse until very smooth. Add the bacon and pulse until just blended.

2. Transfer to a bowl, cover, and refrigerate until the flavors are well integrated, at least one hour or overnight.

3. Serve with apples, vegetables, and/or Wheat Thins.

SERVES 12

GOAL-LINE MASH-UP GUACAMOLE

No real magic here, just the simple glory of avocados, a.k.a. "God's little green butter bombs." Mash a mess of ripe avocados into a chunky paste with tomatoes, onions, and a few distinctively Mexican flavors thrown in for good measure. A subtle and decadent complement to tortilla chips and beer. Lots of chips. Plenty of beer.

SPECIAL NOTE: When the chips run out, as they inevitably do, it is considered acceptable at most tailgates to run one's index finger around the inside of the bowl for those last sublime scoops of green heaven. *Olé!*

THE INGREDIENTS

3 ripe Hass avocados, halved, pitted, and peeled
1/2 ripe tomato, coarsely diced
1/4 cup minced red onion
Juice of 2 limes
2 garlic cloves, peeled and crushed into a paste
2 tablespoons minced fresh cilantro—more if you love the stuff, and I do
1 teaspoon ground cumin
Salt and freshly ground pepper, to taste
1 large bag tortilla chips

THE DRILL

1. In a medium bowl, mash the avocado with a fork until a chunky paste forms. Stir in the tomato, red onion, lime juice, garlic, cilantro, cumin, salt, and pepper until well mixed.

2. If not serving at once, place a sheet of plastic wrap directly on the surface of the guacamole and refrigerate up to three hours.

3. Pass the tortilla chips.

HURRY-UP BLACK BEAN DIP

SERVES
6 TO 8

If you're looking for a near-instant potluck contribution, you just struck pay dirt. It would be tough to make this recipe any simpler — unless you left out the beans. A little chopping, some liquid measure, and a quick *whirrrrrr* of your trusty margarita-maker, and you've got a bowl of ready-to-serve puréed goodness.

THE INGREDIENTS

1 medium red onion, chopped
2 (16-ounce) cans black beans, drained and rinsed
2 tablespoons balsamic vinegar
1 tablespoon fresh orange or lime juice
1 tablespoon chopped fresh cilantro
1 tablespoon olive oil
1 garlic clove, peeled
1 teaspoon ground cumin
Salt and freshly ground pepper, to taste
Tortilla chips and, if you're with that sort of crowd, assorted cut-up raw vegetables

THE DRILL

1. Transfer one tablespoon of the red onion to a cup and set aside for the garnish.

2. In a blender or food processor, puree the beans, remaining red onion, vinegar, orange juice, cilantro, oil, garlic, and cumin.

3. Transfer the dip to a bowl; add salt and pepper. Sprinkle with the reserved red onion and serve with tortilla chips and vegetables.

MAKES 3 HEADS GARLIC

ROASTED GARLIC SPREAD

Whether you're cooking with gas or going the charcoal route, this wrap-ahead dish works as a condiment (smeared on burger buns) or an ingredient **(see Goal Post Roasted Garlic Hummus, p. 55)**. The roasting sweetens the garlic, and, by the time it reaches a paste-like consistency, "the stinking rose" has acquired a surprisingly mellow flavor.

THE INGREDIENTS

3 whole medium heads garlic
I teaspoon olive oil
Salt and freshly ground pepper, to taste

THE DRILL

I. Prepare the grill for a medium fire.

2. With your hands, remove the outer skin from each head of garlic, keeping the heads intact, until there are only a few layers of skin remaining to hold the cloves together. Using a sharp knife or a pair of scissors, cut 1/2 to 3/4 inch off the top of each head (the tops should be flat, with most of the cloves exposed).

2. Place the heads in the center of a 12 x 6-inch sheet of foil. Gather the edge of the foil around the heads so that only the cut tops of the cloves are exposed. Drizzle them with oil, then sprinkle with salt and pepper.

3. Place the packet on the rack along the edge of the grill. Cook until the cloves are very soft and the center is tender when tested with a toothpick, 35 to 45 minutes. Transfer to a plate and let cool. To serve, pull off cloves from each head of garlic and gently squeeze to release the paste. (Can be made ahead of time. Transfer the paste to an airtight container and refrigerate for up to four days.)

WIN·ONE·FOR·THE· DIPPER SPINACH BREAD BOWL

SERVES 4 TO 6

Another page from the quick-mix playbook, this one is served in an edible container. (Read my lips: no cleanup.) The dip's made from precut spinach and a smoothie of cream-style foods. Bloody Mary lovers will recognize the familiar flavor (and sinus rush) of horseradish.

THE INGREDIENTS

1 (8-ounce) package cream cheese, at room temperature
1 (8-ounce) container sour cream
1 cup mayonnaise
1 tablespoon prepared horseradish
1 (1 1/4-ounce) envelope vegetable soup mix
1 (16-ounce) bag frozen chopped spinach, thawed and
    squeezed dry
Assorted crackers and cut-up raw vegetables
1 large, round loaf pumpernickel or sourdough bread

THE DRILL

1. In a large bowl, combine the cream cheese, sour cream, mayonnaise, horseradish, and soup mix, beating with a whisk until well combined. With a rubber spatula, fold in the spinach until blended. Cover and refrigerate until the flavors are blended, at least one hour or overnight.

2. To turn the loaf of bread into a bowl, slice one to two inches off the top. Insert a knife along and around the sides of the loaf to separate the soft innards from a 1-inch-thick crusty border. Scoop out the inside of the loaf to form a bowl and discard the excess bread.

3. Spoon the dip into the bread bowl and serve with the crackers and vegetables.

SERVES 10 TO 12

ANTI-CHOKE ARTICHOKE DIP

Served hot or at room temperature, this version of a holiday classic has green chilies for a little Southwestern kick and plenty of Parmesan cheese for salt and flavor. Serve it with some kind of semi-fancy cracker and watch the guests scrape the dish clean.

THE INGREDIENTS

1 (14-ounce) can artichoke hearts, drained and chopped
1 1/2 cups light mayonnaise
2 (4 1/2-ounce) cans whole green chilies, drained and diced
1 cup shredded Monterey Jack cheese
1 cup grated Parmesan cheese
Couple of shots of hot pepper sauce
Dash of ground red pepper
Crackers, toast, and/or cut-up raw vegetables

THE DRILL

1. Preheat oven to 325°F. In a medium bowl, combine the artichokes, mayonnaise, chilies, Monterey Jack, 1/2 cup of the Parmesan, pepper sauce, and ground red pepper. (For a little more kick, boost the hot pepper sauce and ground red pepper.)

2. Spread the mixture into a shallow 1 1/2-quart baking dish and sprinkle the top with the remaining 1/2 cup of Parmesan. (If you're making the dish ahead of time, at this point cover it with plastic wrap and refrigerate up to one day.)

3. Bake until bubbly and heated through, about 30 minutes. Serve hot with crackers, toast, and/or vegetables.

AUDIBLE
At Step 1, add half a pound or so of cooked crabmeat if there's a special guest you really, really want to impress.

BUCKY BADGER'S ORANGE DIP

SERVES 4 TO 6

For die-hard Wisconsin fans, no gameday party would be complete without a big bowlful of this creamy, slightly mysterious concoction. Though you could conceivably scoop it up with just about anything crunchy — chips, vegetable sticks, crackers — orange dip practically requires the toasted, salty snap of bite-size pretzels. Fans from hot-food conferences can add their own flavorings (chopped jalapeños, say) to boost the zing factor, but the basic recipe embodies down-home Midwestern purity, where cheese and cream are King and Queen.

THE INGREDIENTS

I (8-ounce) package cream cheese, at room temperature
2 tablespoons bottled French salad dressing
1/3 cup ketchup
I tablespoon raw onion, finely minced
1/4 teaspoon salt
Pretzels

THE DRILL

I. In a medium bowl, combine the cream cheese, salad dressing, ketchup, onion, and salt. Cover and let stand at room temperature until the flavors are blended, about an hour.

2. Serve with pretzels. *Only* pretzels. No chips, no crackers, and certainly no veggies.

SERVES 4 TO 6

GOAL POST ROASTED GARLIC HUMMUS

Chances are you've never heard of Ricky Garbanzo, the exceptional 1930s Purdue tailback/botanist who developed the modern chickpea by grafting old-world legumes onto Indiana soybean rootstock. No? Well, that's because I just made him up. I thought this recipe — a great basic Mediterranean dip — deserved a good backstory.

THE INGREDIENTS

1 (15-ounce) can chickpeas, drained
1/4 cup tahini sauce
1/4 cup extra-virgin olive oil, plus more for drizzling
Juice of 2 lemons
8 cloves garlic, roasted* **(or see Roasted Garlic Spread, p. 51)**
4 fresh garlic cloves, peeled and minced — or more to taste
1/2 teaspoon ground cumin
15 good shakes of hot pepper sauce
Kosher salt and freshly ground pepper, to taste
2 tablespoons apple-cider vinegar
Bowl of assorted good-quality olives
Pita bread, cut into wedges

---

*Place a whole head of garlic on a square of aluminum foil. Drizzle with olive oil. Bring corners of foil together and seal loosely. Roast garlic pack in a preheated 350°F oven for 30 minutes. Unused garlic cloves can be saved in a sealed jar and refrigerated.

THE DRILL

1. Put the chickpeas, tahini, 1/4 cup of the oil, and the lemon juice in a food processor and pulse until smooth. Think really thick pancake batter. Add more oil to thin out, if necessary, but be careful not to turn it into soup.

2. Scrape down the sides of the bowl, then add the roasted garlic, fresh garlic, cumin, hot pepper sauce, salt, and ground pepper and pulse until blended.

3. Add the vinegar and pulse until blended.

4. Transfer the hummus to a bowl and drizzle with the remaining oil.

5. Serve with olives and pita bread.

OPTION PLAY

You can skip the roasting and go all the way with raw garlic, but be sure to double up on the postfeast breath mints.

DEEP SOUTH DEVILED EGGS

MAKES 18 DEVILED EGGS

A fixture at pregame festivities at any SEC athletic contest, these little devils are simple to make. For a bit of added showmanship, keep the components (the cooked egg whites and the yolk mixture) separate until you get to the game. Assembling them on-site keeps them from getting watery (and makes it look like you know what you're doing).

THE INGREDIENTS

9 large eggs
1/3 cup mayonnaise (preferably Hellmann's)
1 1/2 tablespoons Dijon mustard
2 teaspoons apple-cider vinegar
Kosher salt and freshly ground pepper, to taste
2 teaspoons scallion (white part only), minced
2 teaspoons fresh tarragon, minced
Paprika, to taste
Tarragon leaves, for garnish

CLASSIC TAILGATING
COLUMBIA, SOUTH CAROLINA

How do you know if you've done something right? When imitators pop up on all sides. In 1990, a bunch of lucky Gamecock fans paid a local developer $45,000 apiece to score a 99-year lease on one of nearly two dozen cabooses parked in the switching yard outside the stadium. Today those gameday digs (living in them is strictly verboten) might well be worth 10 times that—if a Cockaboose Crazy were silly enough to sell the rights to one. No wonder they have developers in rival towns following in their tracks.

THE DRILL

1. In a large saucepan, combine the eggs and enough cold water to cover. Bring to a full boil. When the water reaches a boil, remove the pan from the heat and let the eggs stand, covered, for 18 minutes. Drain the eggs, leaving them in the pan. Add enough cold water to the pan to cover the eggs. Let stand until the eggs are cool enough to handle.

2. Peel the eggs. Cut each egg in half lengthwise. Transfer the yolks to a small bowl and mash well with a fork. Stir in the mayonnaise, mustard, vinegar, salt, and pepper until smooth. Spoon the filling into a zip-top plastic bag and snip one corner of the bag.

3. Arrange the egg whites cut-side-up on a large serving plate. Distribute the scallion and minced tarragon over the cavities. Squeeze out the filling from the bag, piping it into the cavities. Sprinkle the stuffed eggs with paprika and garnish with whole tarragon leaves. Cover with plastic wrap and refrigerate until ready to serve.

ROOKIE MISTAKE

THE ORIGINAL FROSH BONEHEAD PLAY

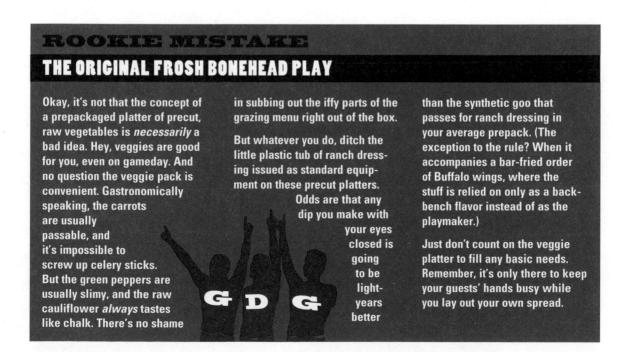

Okay, it's not that the concept of a prepackaged platter of precut, raw vegetables is *necessarily* a bad idea. Hey, veggies are good for you, even on gameday. And no question the veggie pack is convenient. Gastronomically speaking, the carrots are usually passable, and it's impossible to screw up celery sticks. But the green peppers are usually slimy, and the raw cauliflower *always* tastes like chalk. There's no shame in subbing out the iffy parts of the grazing menu right out of the box.

But whatever you do, ditch the little plastic tub of ranch dressing issued as standard equipment on these precut platters. Odds are that any dip you make with your eyes closed is going to be light-years better than the synthetic goo that passes for ranch dressing in your average prepack. (The exception to the rule? When it accompanies a bar-fried order of Buffalo wings, where the stuff is relied on only as a back-bench flavor instead of as the playmaker.)

Just don't count on the veggie platter to fill any basic needs. Remember, it's only there to keep your guests' hands busy while you lay out your own spread.

CHAPTER 4
WHISTLE WETTERS

ALL-WEATHER LIQUID REFRESHMENTS

CHALK TALK

Okay, so you've crafted a simple and flat-out delicious tailgate menu—you still need to make sure that your guests slide effortlessly into the right mood in which to enjoy it. You can be certain of making that happen with flood tides of your favorite strong liquids, along with oceans of bottled water and soda for the nontipplers and/or designated drivers in your party.

Seriously, providing an ice chest full of frosty-cold beverages isn't just a good idea—it's Tailgate Commandment No. 1. But there's no rule that says you should stop with brews. A little creativity in the beverage department can add a whole new dimension to the great vittles that you're starting to crank out.

Branch out beyond the brew-in-a-bottle rut, and you'll be able to explore how simple cocktails, punches, coolers, and hot chocolate can provide effective in-cup climate control, whether you're slathering on sunscreen or howling into the teeth of a pre-kickoff blizzard.

ACC SWEET TEA

SERVES
4 TO 6

Noted North Carolina food writer Fred Thompson is fond of calling this supersweet concoction "the house wine of the South." And to be sure, you'll find some version of sweet tea at just about any Southern college town in the ACC and SEC, as well as in many over in Big 12 country. One warning: Restaurants in the deepest South often lean dangerously close to cloying or even crunchy sweetness in their versions. Not this recipe, though. Here you find the secret behind two quarts of a classic, clear fall cooler that's definitely on the crisp side.

THE INGREDIENTS

6 tea bags*
1/8 teaspoon baking soda (a good pinch)
2 cups boiling water
1 1/2 to 2 cups sugar — or, if you're new to sweet tea,
   1 1/4 cups
6 cups cold water
Ice

THE DRILL

1. Place the tea bags and baking soda in a two-cup glass measure or ceramic teapot. Pour in the boiling water. Cover and let steep for 15 minutes.

2. Remove the tea bags. Note: Don't squeeze the bags (that will add a bitter taste).

3. Pour the tea mixture into a two-quart pitcher. Add the sugar and stir until almost dissolved. Stir in the cold water and cool to room temperature. Cover and refrigerate until thoroughly chilled, about two hours.

4. Pour over ice and serve.

---

*For this and all other tea recipes for tailgates, use ordinary, standard-issue teas, nothing fancy. Go with Lipton not Earl Grey. Think high noon in Oxford, Mississippi, instead of high tea in Oxford, England.

SERVES
4 TO 6

ICED MINT TEA

A nonalcoholic nod to the mint julep, this is the perfect beverage for your designated driver. Fact is, any warm-weather gathering will welcome this cooling iced tea with its little jolt of fresh spearmint.

THE INGREDIENTS

2 quarts cold water
7 black tea bags
12 sprigs fresh spearmint
Zest of 3 lemons, grated
1 1/2 cups sugar
1 cup fresh lemon juice
Ice

THE DRILL

1. Bring one quart of the water to a boil in a medium saucepan. Add the tea bags, spearmint, and lemon zest; cover the pan and remove from the heat. Let the mixture steep for 15 minutes.

2. Strain the mixture through a sieve into a two-quart pitcher. Add the remaining quart of water, sugar, and lemon juice, stirring until the sugar dissolves. Cool to room temperature. Cover and refrigerate until thoroughly chilled, about two hours. Transfer to a thermos, and head on out to the parking lot.

3. Pour over ice and serve.

AUDIBLE

A SUN STROKE OF GENIUS

You can actually replenish your iced tea supplies during a long afternoon tailgate—provided you have a nice, clear day and a bit of patience. Put six tea bags in a two-quart, clear-glass pitcher or container and fill with cold water. Put the lid on the container, or cover the pitcher and let steep in a sunlit spot for three to four hours. Put on ice until thoroughly chilled, about two hours. Pour over ice and serve.

ROOT BEER TO ROOT FOR

SERVES 5 TO 6

Think home-brewing anything that's not beer is a complete waste of time? Well, don't get your hackles up; this beverage is for your little nieces and nephews and cousins by the dozens. A nice, refreshing root beer is a snap and can make you the best uncle (or aunt) ever. Mix the super-concentrated root beer extract with the sugar syrup at home, then add fizzy water at the game.

THE INGREDIENTS

3/4 cup sugar
3/4 cup hot water
1 teaspoon root beer concentrate or extract
1 (1-liter) bottle seltzer water or club soda
Ice

THE DRILL

1. Combine the sugar and hot water in a 1 1/2-quart pitcher, stirring with a whisk until the sugar dissolves into a syrup. Let stand until slightly cooled, about five minutes. Stir in the root beer concentrate until blended.

2. Gradually pour in the seltzer water or club soda.

3. Pour over ice and serve.

SERVES
4

BENCHWARMING HOT CHOCOLATE

Late-season games in the Big Ten, Mountain West, and the Ivys wouldn't be complete without a steaming thermos of creamy hot chocolate. This version is leagues beyond the instant variety, not to mention that it goes a whole lot better with that splash of peppermint schnapps you were thinking about adding.

THE INGREDIENTS

5 cups whole milk
1/4 cup sugar
2 1/2 ounces bittersweet chocolate (such as Scharffen Berger),
    chopped
Large pinch of kosher salt
Whipped cream, for topping
Additional grated bittersweet chocolate (optional)

THE DRILL

1. In a medium saucepan, combine the milk, sugar, chopped chocolate, and salt, and beat with a whisk until blended. Cook over medium heat, whisking gently, until the chocolate melts. Increase the heat to medium-high; whisk more vigorously until the mixture is frothy. Cook just until the mixture forms small bubbles around the edge of the pan (do not bring to a full boil). Remove the pan from the heat.

2. To serve, ladle the hot chocolate into four small mugs, spooning the froth over each. Top each serving with a dollop of whipped cream, and sprinkle with grated chocolate (if using).

CITRUS BOWL LEMONADE

SERVES 4 TO 6

This is a flavorful twist on a classic, made from scratch. (Face it, you're tired of drinking that canned, chemical, yellow-flavor lemon-type drink, aren't you?) The addition of a little fresh ginger and a bit of orange juice provides depth and zing.

THE INGREDIENTS

6 cups cold water
1/2 cup peeled and roughly chopped fresh ginger
1/2 cup honey
1/2 cup fresh lemon juice
1/4 cup fresh orange juice
Ice

THE DRILL

1. Bring two cups of the water to a boil in a small saucepan. Add ginger and honey. Cover pan and remove from heat. Let mixture steep 30 minutes.

2. Strain the mixture through a sieve into a two-quart pitcher, pressing on the solids with the back of a spoon. Stir in remaining four cups of water, lemon juice, and orange juice. Cool to room temperature. Cover and refrigerate until thoroughly chilled, about two hours.

3. Pour over ice and serve.

PLAYMAKER

A CELEBRATORY SPIKE

For an adult twist to the classic summer refresher, add a little vodka. Put 2½ cups of a freshly made lemonade (like the one above), 10 ounces of your favorite lemon-flavor vodka, and the juice and shells of two lemons into a one-quart thermos. Cover and shake to blend thoroughly. Serve over ice. The combination of tart and sweet gives this drink a taste reminiscent of the line between late adolescence and grown-up responsibility. You are 21, aren't you?

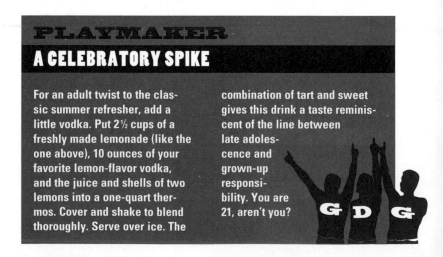

ROCKIN' MARGARITAS

Margaritas are far and away the most popular tequila drink. But in the wrong hands, they can taste like the bastard child of Everclear grain alcohol and a chalky lime Kool-Aid. To avoid this fate, mix up a thermos full of this baby at home, add a little ice when you get to the game, and shake to chill.

THE INGREDIENTS

1 1/2 cups fresh lime juice
1 1/2 cups (12 ounces) white tequila
3/4 cup (6 ounces) triple sec
Kosher salt (optional)
Ice
6 lime twists

THE DRILL

1. In a one-quart thermos, combine the lime juice, tequila, and triple sec. Close the thermos and shake vigorously.

2. Salt or no salt? Pose the question before the next step so the salt people can prep their own glasses using the kosher salt.

3. To serve, add a handful of ice to the thermos, close and shake again. Fill the glasses with ice. Pour in the 'ritas, and garnish each with a lime twist.

BUILDING A GAMEDAY BAR

Once you've graduated from college, the glamour of flammable jungle juices, ice luges, and double-barrel beer bongs mostly fades away. Thank goodness. But somehow, sometimes, we revert to some of our primal cocktail experiences. We're not talking about fancy, shaken-not-stirred martinis, but the simple, flask-and-fizzy combos that work just fine on any game day.

For outdoor gatherings, pack along an extra card table, an empty cooler for bottle transport, and — bingo! — you've got a bar that can cater to any basic taste. Add multiple bags of ice to the mix, and you're in business.

The usual two-ingredient highballs (bourbon and Coke, gin and tonic, Seven and Seven) appeal to just about everybody, and with the right options — don't forget the diet soda — along with plenty of beer, you'll be hailed as an All-American *GameDay* gourmet.

Liquors

Bourbon

Gin

Rum

Tequila

Vodka

Wine*

Red

White

Beer

Duh

Mixers

Bottled Bloody Mary mix

Club soda

Cola (regular and diet)

Extra-strong ginger beer

Lemon/lime soda (regular and diet)

Orange juice

Tonic water

Garnishes

Cut lemons and limes

Olives

Pickled okra or spiced green beans (for Bloody Marys)

*This isn't the time or place to try to impress anyone with your favorite, precious 1982 Bordeaux. Just about anything domestic in the $10–12 range will fit the bill nicely.

FUMBLE-PROOF FROZEN MARGARITAS

SERVES 8

Early-season football games in the Sun Belt often require something more bracing than a frosty brew. (Hard to believe, isn't it?) This simple-yet-bulletproof recipe for frozen margaritas is the next best thing to a swimming pool on a hundred-degree July afternoon. Truly dedicated fans will splurge for a gasoline-powered blender to prepare these cold Mexican treats at the tailgate. The rest of us will be content to mix them at home and pour into a prechilled thermos.

THE INGREDIENTS

I (6-ounce) can Minute Maid frozen Limeade[1]
I 1/2 cups white tequila[2]
3/4 cup triple sec[3]
Ice, preferably bagged[4]
8 lime wedges

THE DRILL

I. Empty Limeade into your trusty blender. Add the other liquids, using the empty Limeade can as a measuring cup. (I use one can of tequila and one-third of a can of triple sec to make a perfect drink, if I do say so myself.) Set blender on "churn" and gently mix, about 10 seconds. Pack the blender to the top with ice, and set to "stun." Whir until the ice chunks turn to slush.

2. Once the chunks have been blended smooth, pour a smidgeon of the resulting elixir into an appropriate drinking receptacle — say, a thermal cup? — add a lime wedge, and sample the fruits of your labor.

more

---

[1] I use Minute Maid because it's consistently balanced (sweet/tart) without a lot of artificial coloring. Grocery store off-brands tend to use green food coloring, which makes the final product look like frozen engine coolant.

[2] Don't skimp on tequila quality. Avoid cheaper brands named after random Mexican icons (Sombrero, El Borracho, or La Bamba). Invest the extra two bucks in a mid-grade silver tequila from one of the familiar distilleries (Sauza Blanco or Jose Cuervo Clásico, *por ejemplo*).

[3] If you have to cut corners, do it here. I just haven't been able to justify moving up to one of the better orange liqueurs (Grand Marnier, Cointreau). General guideline: Avoid bottles bearing the names of major oil refineries. Other than that, anything goes.

[4] Grab a bag of ice at the nearest convenience store instead of depending on homemade cubes. Machine-made cubes tend toward the tiny, and the smaller the cubes, the quicker the blend.

PLAYMAKER
THE ALL-PURPOSE THERMOS BOTTLE

Most of the beverage recipes in *GameDay Gourmet* have been tailored to pour into insulated beverage containers, a.k.a. the shatterproof big brother of those all-too-fragile lunch box thermoses we all grew up with. Whether you're keeping hot chocolate piping or frozen margaritas on the slushy side, this industrial-strength thermal cooler is a great all-around beverage container. It clocks in at just over a quart (40 ounces, actually), which is just enough to get a party off the ground—even one with its fair share of cocktail enthusiasts. And the bulletproof, industrial appearance isn't just skin-deep: You can pretty much do anything to it short of crushing it under an RV. And besides, even if your day job requires a suit and tie, this baby will make you feel like a girder-walking badass.

G D G

3. Take two sips very quickly, the better to savor the sweet, stabbing pain of margarita-induced Freezer Head. Sure, it hurts like hell, but at least the taste will compensate.

4. Pour the remainder into a big thermos and head on out to the stadium. Or if you're worried about global warming melting your wonderful concoction, herd everyone into your rec room and watch the game on TV. Think of your coffee table as a tailgate.

**SERVES
4 TO 6**

BLOODY SATURDAY BLOODY MARYS

For those of you concerned about your health (you know who you are), think of the Bloody Mary as a vodka-enhanced salad in a glass that will benefit any late night pre-party or early-morning tailgate. Our version is spiked with enough hot sauce and horseradish to wake the sleepiest of taste buds. Vegetarians take note: This particular Bloody's rich flavor comes from a touch of beef broth. Nowhere is it written (certainly not here) that you can't ask for one without.

THE INGREDIENTS

2 1/2 cups good-quality tomato juice
I cup vodka
1/4 cup fresh lemon juice
2 teaspoons prepared horseradish, drained
I teaspoon beef broth
I teaspoon hot pepper sauce
I teaspoon Worcestershire sauce
Ice
4 lime wedges
4 stuffed green olives
4 celery stalks
4 shrimp, cooked, shelled, and deveined, with tails
    intact (optional)

THE DRILL

I. In a one-quart thermos, combine the tomato juice, vodka, lemon juice, horseradish, broth, pepper sauce, and Worcestershire sauce. Stir to combine, and close the thermos.

2. Pour over ice to serve. Garnish each serving with a lime wedge, an olive, a celery stalk, and shrimp (if using).

DOUBLE SECRET SANGRIA

SERVES 10 TO 12

Like all punch-style drinks, sangria brings an air of fun and surprise to any tailgate. Wine is the main event, of course, but there's no bottle to read, no cork to sniff, and no room for snobbery. This easy recipe comes from recreational mixologist Stephen Este, who concocted it for summer-night parties in central Texas. It's far from highbrow — the secret ingredient is orange soda, after all — but if you get it plenty cold and float in some fresh fruit, all the beer-haters will beat a path to your tailgate.

THE INGREDIENTS

2 bottles dry red wine
1 (2-liter) bottle orange soda
Fresh orange, lemon, lime, apple, and/or peach slices
Fresh lemon or orange juice, to taste
Ice

THE DRILL

1. In a large thermos or pitcher, combine the wine and soda.

2. Stir in the fruit slices and the juice.

3. Cover and refrigerate until thoroughly chilled, about two hours.

4. Pour over ice and serve.

NO CHAMPAGNE, NO GAIN

Looking for an excuse to break out the champagne? Take your pick: Homecoming ... A bowl invite that's on the line ... A shot at breaking that nasty, seven-game losing streak ... Gameday falling on a Saturday ... Just because. You can get five healthy glasses of plain bubbly out of every bottle, and your guests will sing your praises. But you will turn the day into a truly special occasion by making each glass into a spiffy champagne cocktail. If you have the right stuff on hand, that is: orange juice, for a mimosa; cranberry juice, lime juice, and a splash of an orange liqueur like Grand Marnier for a champagne cosmo; pomegranate juice and lemon-flavor vodka for a poinsettia; and crème de cassis for a kir royale. Just pour some champagne into a flute (don't even think about using anything but a real, honest-to-god *glass* glass), and, employing the rough ratio of 3 parts champagne to one part flavoring, create your guest's cocktail of preference.

G D G

SERVES 8

LSU TIGER'S MILK PUNCH

The lovely Elise Decoteau is a dedicated LSU fan who keeps several gallons of this versatile punch-style cocktail in her freezer at all times. During the summer, it's a sweet, soothing slush with a subtle hint of whiskey. Later in the season, the assertive flavors — bourbon, vanilla, nutmeg — make you think of the impending holidays, even if your team won't be getting invited to a bowl game.

THE INGREDIENTS

1/2 gallon whole milk
2 1/2 to 3 cups confectioners' sugar, or to taste
1 1/2 cups (12 ounces) bourbon whiskey
1 tablespoon vanilla extract
Ice
Ground nutmeg

THE DRILL

1. In a large pitcher, combine the milk and confectioners' sugar, and beat with a whisk until the sugar is dissolved. Stir in the bourbon and vanilla. Pour into a large, airtight container (such as a half-gallon milk jug), cover and freeze overnight or even up to a month.

2. The morning of the tailgate, let the punch thaw at room temperature for at least two hours. Pour into a large thermos or straight from the jug. Pour over ice to serve, and top each serving with a pinch of nutmeg.

CLASSIC TAILGATING

BATON ROUGE, LOUISIANA

The loudest venue in college football is also home to the nation's most extreme tailgating scene. On home Saturdays, rabid fans from every corner of this food-crazy state converge on Tiger Stadium, setting up industrial deep fryers, rocket-powered crawfish boilers, and whole-hog roasting boxes. There's so much food and drink even the visiting fans get to eat for free.

KIRK HERBSTREIT: "SEC schools generally take things to a whole other tailgating level, but LSU stands out. Acres filled with hundreds of RVs, the air full of emissions from the smokers and grills the size of pickup trucks."

CHRIS FOWLER: "LSU is something to see. Nobody wants to play there at night, if only because they know the fans will be well-percolated and that much more intense."

HOTTY TODDY (GOSH A'MIGHTY)

SERVES 6

Who the hell are we? Hey! Ole Miss fans seem to find just about any excuse to break into their trademark fight chant, which also means that they've probably been partaking of this belly-warming winter cocktail. After a few soothing sips, inhibitions loosen, and it's *Flim-flam, bim-bam, Ole Miss by damn!*

THE INGREDIENTS

6 sugar cubes
2 1/4 cups boiling water
1 1/2 cups (12 ounces) bourbon whiskey
6 lemon slices
Grated nutmeg

THE DRILL

1. Rinse a one-quart thermos with scalding-hot water. Drain and add the sugar cubes.

2. Stir in the boiling water and bourbon until the sugar dissolves. Close the thermos.

3. To serve, pour the toddy into six coffee cups, then top each with a lemon slice and a pinch of nutmeg.

THE BOTTLED-IN BOILERMAKER

If you look deep into the glazed, fiberglass eyes of Purdue Pete, the university's eponymous mascot, you might think that before taking the field he had quite a few of these classic beer-and-a-shot combos. (It's worth mentioning that the real Purdue mascot, the Boilermaker Special, is a Victorian-era locomotive that's managed to resist the cutesy "Thomas the Tank Engine" treatment since it debuted in 1940.)

A traditional boilermaker is a shot of bourbon or sour mash whiskey served with a beer chaser. Combining the basics is a matter of taste, as drinkers generally adhere to either the "swig and chug" school or the "plop and slam" method (which entails dropping the full shot into the beer glass, then speedily slurping the whole shebang down.)

Out at the stadium, however, as well as flavorwise, you would probably be better off bringing along a hip flask of whiskey and a bottle or can of your favorite brew. Take a few sips of the beer to make some room, then add a few glugs of the brown stuff. You'll get all the fizz of your beer with a customized whiskey kick.

CHAPTER 5 ⟜

FIRE DRILL

GRILLING AND
THE ESSENCE
OF BARBECUE

CHALK TALK

Get within a half-mile of any stadium parking lot on gameday, and several of your senses will pick up the presence of the tailgater's trademark cooking method: the charcoal grill. A thin haze of gray-blue smoke hovers over the sea of parked cars and RVs. Step a little closer, and the smell of roasting meats — burgers, birds, sausages, and chops — reaches your brain's pleasure centers. Get close enough to see the cooks at work, and you'll hear the sizzle of meaty treats being licked by flames, a sound guaranteed to make your taste buds reflexively kick into overdrive.

The trusty backyard grill — charcoal or propane-powered, your choice — is the most popular cooking method for parking-lot tailgaters, hands down. Simple to use and familiar to just about every American male, the grill conjures memories of backyard cookouts and Fourth of July picnics during hot-weather games and provides hand-warming heat during the later part of the football schedule.

Pack a grill, grab a few pounds of ground meat from the fridge, score a case of beer, and you've already got the makings of a pregame gathering.

But after a few games, would-be meat masters realize that cooking great grilled food means more than just squirting briquettes with a gallon of flammable fluid and touching it off with mom's Zippo. There's a thin line between a perfectly seared, Fowlerized fillet (see **Fowler Family Steak Marinade, p. 91**) dripping with natural juices and a sooty puck of overcooked chuck.

But with a little practice and an equal amount of imagination, any aspiring burger flipper can learn the subtle art of the outdoor grill — skills that carry over to any cooking venue. And to cap it off, it's a socially acceptable way to live out any kid's early fantasy of playing with fire without getting screamed at by an overprotective parent. (We're looking at *you*, Mom...)

TRUE BARBECUE VS. GRILLING

Every tailgater worth his or her giant foam cowboy hat should know the difference between barbecue and grilling. The two terms are used interchangeably in many cases, much to the chagrin of the entire Southeastern Conference, fans of most Texas teams, and chunks of the urban Midwest. In these areas, barbecue talk can take on near-religious overtones and fuels plenty of off-season regional rivalries.

And if you doubt this, get a North Carolina Tar Heel to talk with a Texas Longhorn about barbecue. Then run like hell.

Grilling is a direct, high-heat cooking process that sears meat or vegetables rather quickly, sealing in the juices and making those fashionable black lines that the kids like so much. If you grew up thinking of salmon steaks seared on a Weber as barbecue or referring to the backyard appliance as the barbecue grill, please recalibrate your brain.

Real **barbecue** (or bar-b-que, or BBQ) requires a well-tended hardwood fire, plenty of indirect heat, about 12 hours of constant

attention, and, preferably, a
recognizable animal (a whole
hog, a flock of chickens, a
side o' beef) as the smokee.
After hours and hours of
slow smoking, the meat's
connective tissue pretty
much disappears, and every
strand of flesh is perfumed
with magical flavor. Which,

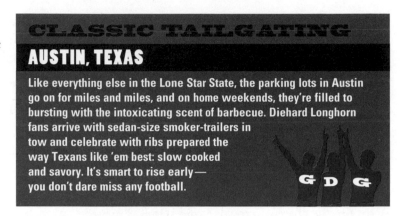

of course, is why barbecue fans fight for their regional barbecue
style (pig cooked over hickory, beef over oak, ribs with a dry rub)
as readily as for their old alma mater.

True barbecue requires a good deal of time, attention, and firewood—
not exactly what you want for the average gameday feast unless you've
got a *lot* of available sick days at work. For our basic purposes, we'll
concentrate on basic grilling methods and combinations in which a long,
slow session in the oven can mimic some of the texture, if not all of the
flavor, of a long, slow smoke.

GRILLING BASICS

Whether your menu plans include a monstrous rack of *Flintstones*-size
beef ribs, your sister-in-law's marinated chicken skewers, or a pack of
fluorescent pink, store-brand hot dogs, there are a few basic skills that
can improve your "high heat zone" performance.

I. Know Your Grill

Aside from the professional tailgaters who show up at the game towing
30-foot, custom-welded, portable kitchen trailers, most folks cook on
the same charcoal or gas grills that are standard equipment on suburban

patios. Charcoal setups are more portable and provide a bit of smoky flavor but require more cleanup after the party's done. Gas versions spark up quickly and offer plenty of turn-the-dial heat control but can be a bear to transport for folks without pickup trucks. And make sure you've read the manufacturer's instructions before that first satisfying *fooooshhhh!* Seriously. You might even learn something.

2. Kick the Starter

A tip for the charcoal crowd: Avoid standard pressed-sawdust briquettes and bottles of nasty-tasting lighter fluid. Mix two kinds of bagged charcoal — the presoaked, easy-light variety and a pricier, all-hardwood kind — and you'll get a good blend of quick-light convenience and smoky flavor.

3. Play the Zones

Whether your grill is powered by hardwood charcoal or propane gas, it's best to have a three-zone setup for backyard cooking. Mentally divide the grill into thirds: One "high heat" zone for searing and fast cooking, one for less intense, "low heat" cooking, and the remaining "indirect heat" zone for resting and recovery. (If you're doing a slow-cook barbecue, you'll need to assemble a drip pan. Place a disposable foil roasting pan in the indirect heat zone, fill the pan with about two cups of water,

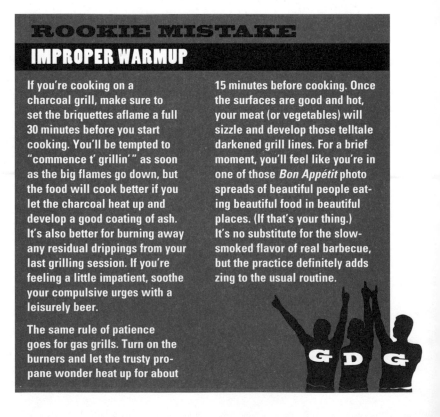

ROOKIE MISTAKE
IMPROPER WARMUP

If you're cooking on a charcoal grill, make sure to set the briquettes aflame a full 30 minutes before you start cooking. You'll be tempted to "commence t' grillin'" as soon as the big flames go down, but the food will cook better if you let the charcoal heat up and develop a good coating of ash. It's also better for burning away any residual drippings from your last grilling session. If you're feeling a little impatient, soothe your compulsive urges with a leisurely beer.

The same rule of patience goes for gas grills. Turn on the burners and let the trusty propane wonder heat up for about 15 minutes before cooking. Once the surfaces are good and hot, your meat (or vegetables) will sizzle and develop those telltale darkened grill lines. For a brief moment, you'll feel like you're in one of those *Bon Appétit* photo spreads of beautiful people eating beautiful food in beautiful places. (If that's your thing.) It's no substitute for the slow-smoked flavor of real barbecue, but the practice definitely adds zing to the usual routine.

PLAYMAKER
ESSENTIAL GRILL TOOLS

LOCKING TONGS

A sturdy grill spatula might be good for flipping burgers, but for just about any other food on the grill or in the skillet—ribs, poultry parts, sausages—a good pair of metal tongs is a much more practical tool. Well-made tongs act as an extension of your hand, allowing you to manipulate, check, rearrange, and turn foods with a lot more precision than with a spatula, which is pretty much limited to a scrape-and-flip motion.

SILICONE BASTING BRUSH

A new entry in the "grill master's best friend" category, a silicone brush features stubby, flexible bristles made of heat-resistant silicone. This little baby rinses off clean and won't burn up if you drop it on the grill.

INSTANT-READ THERMOMETER

This is the most reliable way to tell if larger cuts of meat are actually cooked through. Unless you've got a lot of experience with the grill, these little poke-and-check devices are great for getting smoking times just right. Otherwise, you run the risk of overcooking (or worse, *under*cooking) the pregame meaty treats you've worked so hard to serve.

FIRE EXTINGUISHER

Always good to have around, just in case things get a little too hot. Keep it charged and readily accessible, for safety's sake.

SILICONE OVEN MITTS

Another heat-resistant wonder that's about as durable as it gets. If only so you don't have to ruin your favorite winter cap or shirt sleeve transporting a hot dish from place to place.

then cover with the grill rack.) On a charcoal pit, stack two-thirds of your preheated coals under the high heat zone, the remaining coals under the low zone, and leave the indirect heat zone empty. On a gas grill, simply adjust the burners to achieve the same multizone effect.

Different heat levels give you more control over the grilling process—if sausages are cooking too quickly, move them to a cooler zone for a slower roast.

4. Dealing With Flare-Ups and Other Fireside Dramas

Even though fat is any food lover's friend, it can cause sudden (and potentially painful) flare-ups on the grill. It's a good policy to have a spray bottle filled with water handy for just those occasions. Shooting flames can also char the outside of your meats, so move them over to the low heat zone when flare-ups start.

5. Give It a Rest

After your flame-seared masterpiece comes off the grill, resist the temptation to dig in immediately. Instead, cover the fresh-grilled lovelies with foil, and drink a 10-minute beer. "But it's done, and I'm *hungry*— why wait?" you ask, banging your fists on the nearest folding table. When your meat's on a grill, all the precious, flavorful juices migrate toward the center, away from the fire. A few minutes of cooling allows the meat's natural gravy to redistribute. The result is better, juicier meat instead of a puddle on your plate.

GOOD D
WHAT TO OFFER THE EXTREMELY PICKY EATER

Sometimes the call of the grill requires that you move beyond the barnyard. (Just ask University of Washington fans, who routinely find themselves with a freezer full of salmon when football season rolls around.) So if you're looking to mix it up a bit, remember that our finny friends can add some punch to traditional football fare.

Simple fish fillets are a great emergency backup dish for any outdoor gathering and a good defense against the Extremely Picky Eater. ("Can't eat beef, pork, OR chicken? No problem ... ") With a flick of the wrist, you can throw a premade foil packet on the grill and be a culinary hero in about 15 minutes.

The easiest way to grill fish doesn't involve grilling at all—it's a foil-packet version of the French technique *en papillote* (which translates loosely to "in paper"). Recovering Boy Scouts might also recognize this metallic variation from their campfire cooking merit badge requirements.

This method won't dry out the delicate fish because it's not really grilling. The packet makes a self-contained steamer that cooks with no pan, no boiling water, and no real cleanup concerns (all you gotta do is wad up the foil and toss it away).

Just lay out a couple of sheets of heavy-duty foil, slap a slab of fish down, add some lemon or simple spices, and fold that sucker up into a tight envelope. Fifteen minutes on the grill (or in your home oven at 375°F), and the fish cooks up moist and tasty.

ROOKIE MISTAKE

GREASED LIGHTNING ON THE RACK

This tip involves a pretty standard nonstick maneuver—something that would be easy to do on the stove but gets trickier on the grill. The idea is simple: Get a thin layer of oil between the scorching metal grate and your cooking cow flesh. If you can get a little edible lube on the grill before slapping the patties down, you'll leave less of the caramelized crust behind when you flip 'em over. More crust means a better burger, every time.

If you were using a stove-top skillet, all you'd have to do is spritz the cooking surface with nonstick cooking spray. But spraying vegetable oil onto a hot pan is *completely* different from squirting the same stuff onto open flames. Remember the hairspray-and-lighter trick from third grade? Same principle here: You are essentially making

a household flamethrower. The bottom line: A quick spritz can lead to singed arm hair and even a possible ambulance ride. Best not to use the spray product. (*FIRST DISCLAIMER for those who can't read between the lines: DO NOT TRY THIS AT HOME. YOU'VE BEEN WARNED.*)

The key is to take a clean (yet disposable) cotton dishcloth and rip it into four pieces. Fold the quarter towel into a tight wad o' cloth, and douse it in vegetable oil until it's damp. (No polyester blends here—you don't want a mouth full of molten plastic with your burgers, do you?)

Using long-handled metal tongs (the grill master's

friend), rub the hot grill rack *immediately* before putting the burgers on the grill. Take care not to push too hard on the towel, as the oil might drip on the coals and flare up. No worse than with a fatty bratwurst, but still. Better safe than sorry.

SECOND DISCLAIMER: EXERCISE EXTREME CAUTION during this process. Work fast and GET THE CLOTH CLEAR OF OPEN FLAMES AS SOON AS POSSIBLE. If you don't have good tongs, then forget it until you can pick up a pair. Greasing the rack makes a big difference in your finished product, but not if it means living with second-degree burger burns.

G D G

CHICKEN
WHY SKIN AND BONES ARE BETTER

In the world of tailgate grilling, chicken is a necessary evil. On average, chicken is comparatively bland, tough to cook well, and takes about twice as long as your favorite red-meat treats (burgers, steaks, pork chops, and sausage-type devices).

But at every grill-centric tail-gate, roughly half the guests will request or bring along some form of the trusty yard bird as their main course. And pretty often, *all* of these poultry-pickers will be women. So do the math. If you wanna impress the gals, you need to have a couple of fire-kissed chicken dishes in your repertoire.

It's also good to know how to take extra care with our free-range friends. Even if your guests aren't hip to the bacterial risks of America's favorite edible bird, you need to be.

When you're standing in your grocer's meat aisle, shopping for tailgate supplies, there's a tempta-tion to buy the thing that *looks* to be the easiest, most patty-like cut of chicken: the skinless, boneless breast (hereafter known as the SBB). All you gotta do is slap 'em on the grill, and *voilà!*—chicken burgers, no?

No. The chicken's white meat is loved by many because it's low in fat and mild in flavor—in other words, the tofu of the meat world—but cook it over direct heat, and it quickly gets tough and chewy. With SBB, there's nothing to protect the delicate meat (no fat, no juice, no skin), so it grills up all rubbery—no matter *what* the commercials say.

So resist the chicken burger urge and make a beeline to the Family Paks of whole breasts (bone in, skin on). You'll recognize these from countless childhood chicken buckets and their many other TV appearances. Actual chicken breasts are a better deal because of their protective layer of skin and bony substructure. The skin keeps the fire out and the moisture and residual fats inside the meat itself. The bone transmits radiant heat from the coals, helping to cook the breast evenly. A real breast might not be cooked as consistently as the SBB, but the flavor and texture are more than worth it.

Rub the breasts with salt and pepper or your favorite spice mix, then let them roast long and slow on the medium-to-low zone of your grill. During the last 10 min-utes or so of grilling, baste them with a good barbecue sauce. (Why wait to add the sauce? You wouldn't want the residual sugar to burn over high heat, now, would you?)

SERVES
4 TO 6

WOLFPACK BEER CAN CHICKEN

Often referred to by an alternate, less polite moniker ("beer butt chicken"), this simple recipe combines a traditional spice-rubbed technique with a somewhat unorthodox grilling platform: an upended, half-full can of beer. Fans at NC State give their roasting birds a bit of a bite by spritzing the skin with apple cider vinegar. As with all "whole bird" recipes, make sure you bring along a suitable carving blade (a chef's knife will do nicely) and a big cutting board used only for poultry (to cut down the possibility of bacterial cross-contamination). Better safe than sorry, dontcha know.

THE INGREDIENTS

1 (4-pound) whole chicken
1 tablespoon vegetable oil
1 (12-ounce) can beer
Apple cider vinegar in a spray bottle

For the spice rub:
1 tablespoon sugar
1 teaspoon kosher salt
1 teaspoon mustard powder
1 teaspoon onion powder
1 teaspoon garlic powder
1 teaspoon paprika
1/2 teaspoon ground coriander
1/2 teaspoon ground cumin
1/2 teaspoon freshly ground black pepper

THE DRILL

1. Oil the grill rack. Prepare the grill for indirect heat (see Grilling Basics, Play the Zones, p. 80).

2. To make the spice rub, combine all the ingredients in a small bowl. Remove the neck, giblets, and any excess fat from the chicken. Rinse the chicken and drain; pat dry with paper towels. Brush the oil over the chicken. Sprinkle the spice rub inside the main cavity and over the skin.

more ☞

3. Open the beer can and pour off half the beer. (Of course, most people wouldn't waste it — they would drink it themselves.) Set the half-full can on your countertop, and, holding the chicken upright, place it over the can so that the can goes into the body cavity. Pull the chicken legs forward to form a sort of tripod, allowing the chicken to sit upright over the can. Transfer the chicken to the grill rack over the drip pan, keeping the can upright (the legs of the chicken need to touch the grill rack to maintain stability). Cover and grill, spraying the bird with vinegar every 15 minutes or so, until an instant-read thermometer inserted into a thigh registers 180°F, in about 1 1/4 to 1 1/2 hours.

4. Carefully transfer the chicken and the can to a cutting board (careful, the beer can will be very hot). Let the chicken rest on the can for about 10 minutes. Holding the can with an oven mitt, insert a large fork into the neck of the chicken and lift, removing the can from chicken. Cut the chicken into serving pieces.

ROOKIE MISTAKE

CHICKEN CARE 101

Every 800-pound griller should know that chicken requires a little extra care when it comes to handling and cleanup. Suffice it to say that the clear, watery fluids that come out of a raw chicken can make you *reeeeeeally* sick if you're not careful. So break with tradition and wash your hands, cutting boards, knives, and serving dishes after they've been touched by the bird.

Put it like this: You should be FIVE TIMES MORE CAREFUL with raw chicken than you would be with other food. After all, you don't want your tailgate tribe to get a powerful case of food poisoning before the game starts.

And if you decide to marinate your bird parts, resist the temptation to use that same batch of liquid to baste the cooking chicken. No reason to take chances with presoaked bacteria.

FIRE UP THE MASCOT

As anyone who's seen *The Brady Bunch* can tell you, stealing a mascot is a great way to get someone's goat—sometimes literally. But tailgaters can take the indignity one step further and actually eat their rival's mascot. No, we're not advising you to slow-roast Uga the Georgia Bulldog. But you can indulge in a kind of symbolic devouring. After all, why go through the hassle of actually kidnapping, butchering, and barbecuing Bevo the Texas Longhorn when 100 pounds of grade-A sirloin makes a convenient—and tasty—stand-in? South Carolina Gamecock fans are used to being taunted with plates of fried chicken when they encroach on enemy tailgating territory. And you can bet that when the Arkansas Razorbacks come to town, SEC opponents have plenty of pig sizzling away symbolically. Fortunately, for those looking to make a statement with their parking lot spread, college football is packed with edible mascots of all stripes. Sometimes, all it takes is a little imagination—and an adventurous palate—to make your point.

OFFENSIVE FOWL (CHICKEN, TURKEY, ETC.)
From the proud eagle to the humble duck, birds are popular collegiate mascots. Fortunately, plucked and slapped on a grill, they all roughly look—and taste—like chicken, so feel free to substitute away.

Examples: Blue Hens (Delaware), Cardinals (Louisville), Ducks (Oregon), Eagles (Boston College, Auburn), Falcons (Air Force), Gamecocks (South Carolina), Jayhawks (Kansas), Owls (Rice, Temple), Pelicans (Tulane), Turkeys (Virginia Tech)

Suggested Torching Method: Wolfpack Beer Can Chicken (p. 85)

THE BACK FIELD (PORK, BEEF, ETC.)
You know those charts divvying up a cow into all its edible parts? Nothing gets left over, does it? Your larger, grazing type of collegiate mascot can generously provide everything from ribs to chops to burgers for your tailgating pleasure. And once the meat's on a bun or dripping with sauce, who's going to know if that's *actually* horse or a beefier stand-in?

Examples: Bison (Bucknell), Buffaloes (Colorado), Goats (Navy), Horses (SMU, USC, Boise State), Longhorns (Texas), Mules (Army), Rams (Colorado State, Cornell), Razorbacks (Arkansas)

Suggested Torching Methods: Laura's Old Mountain Jug London Broil (p. 90), The All-American Burger (p. 88), Hickory Stick Pulled Pork Barbecue (p. 94), Jayhawk Double-Clutch Pork Ribs (p. 97)

SPECIAL TEAMS (VARIETY MEATS)
Adventurous tailgaters can add some thrill to their grill with these exotic mascots. Louisiana cooks aren't shy about cooking alligator tail (fried or stewed). Turtle soup shows up on the menu in some coastal areas. Desert dwellers usually have a line on rattlesnake meat. Golden gopher or badger backstrap? You're on your own.

Examples: Bears (Cal, UCLA, Baylor), Beavers (Oregon State), Frogs (Texas Christian), Gators (Florida), Gophers (Minnesota), Rattlesnakes (Florida A&M), Terrapins (Maryland), Wahoo, a type of mackerel (Virginia)

Suggested Torching Methods: Union Bay Salmon (p. 104), Wolfpack Beer Can Chicken (p. 85)—because, you know, everything tastes like chicken.

KIRK'S GATOR TALE
"I don't know if gator meat is a common thing down in Knoxville," Kirk Herbstreit says, "but it's everywhere on gameday when the Vols play Florida. To me, it tastes like chicken, but I guess that's not the point."

THE ALL-AMERICAN BURGER

Admit it: Every time you fire up the grill, you get a craving for a big, juicy burger. Despite the upscale trend in tailgate grilling (lobster? Rustic pizza? C'mon, people!!), we always boomerang back to the classics. And even though we can get a burger from a million drive-through restaurants on damned near any corner, there's something inspiring about a gridiron full of sizzling, grill-marked beef patties.

Burgers are so fundamental that they don't require a recipe as such. You get ground beef, mix in some spices, and shape it into patties. But just because burgers are simple to make doesn't mean they can't be improved upon. A few simple techniques can help perk up this elemental outdoor feast and set you apart from the guy at the next tent flipping gray, overcooked hockey pucks to his friends. If you make a few good choices on the front side, you'll come out with a tastier final product.

I. Choose Chuck

Don't waste your money on preformed pucks or suspiciously labeled "ground meat"—these can contain a *lot* of fat and mystery additives. (Don't even ask. You don't want to know.) The best burger meat is ground chuck (a specific cut), with about 20% fat. Overall, it's a good mix of lean, flavorful meat with a high juice potential.

2. Mix Your Own Meat

If you're going to spice your ground meat — and you really should — don't just sprinkle the patties as they cook. Take a few minutes and knead the salt, ground pepper, or your favorite Cajun seasoning blend through the meat before forming the patties; the flavors will mix with the juices a lot better. Just be careful not to overwork your meat (insert your own suggestive frat house joke here) — a few mushes should be enough to get the spices mixed in without making the patties tough. If the mixture starts to blend smooth, the patties won't be as juicy when they hit the buns. (Insert second joke here.)

3. Puckin' Around

In our mind's eye and in *all* the fast food ads, the perfect burger is always a flat, beefy hockey puck that acts as a perfect platform for goopy cheese, slabs of tomato, and other saucy substances. But as any grizzled grill veteran knows, most backyard patties are shaped more like UFOs—thinner on the edges, with domed centers. In more extreme cases, the burgers are ball-shape hunks o' cow. Tasty? Sure, but hardly the tailgater's dream.

The way to compensate for "flying saucer syndrome" is to shape your patties into standard puck form, then press down on the center with your three middle fingers or the bottom of a pint glass. Don't get carried away—all you want to do is create a quarter-inch divot in the middle of each patty. (Think back to your last game of golf, Sparky.) Done right, the slightly bowl-shaped center will level off as the meat cooks. The result is a picture-perfect patty and the burger of your dreams.

AUDIBLE
SPICING THE PATTY

Though you don't need a formal recipe for the basic burger, here are a few different spicing options. You should always put a little salt and freshly ground pepper into the mix—about one teaspoon of salt and half a teaspoon of pepper per pound of meat—but crack into your spice rack for a little more variety. For more experimental flavors, give these a try:

• 1 teaspoon each of ground cumin and chili powder for a Mexican touch.

• 4 minced garlic cloves and 1 teaspoon of dried basil for Italian zing.

• About 10 pitted kalamata olives, finely chopped, and 1 teaspoon of dried oregano for a Greeky tang.

LAURA'S OLD MOUNTAIN JUG LONDON BROIL

SERVES 6 TO 8

Though it might not be a rivalry between traditional powerhouse teams, the contest between the Western Carolina Catamounts and Appalachian State Mountaineers packs a wallop in Carolina mountain circles. Laura Thompson and her daddy, Fred, fix up this savory grilled steak to cheer on WCU during their yearly battle.

THE INGREDIENTS

1 (3-pound) top round steak (London broil)
2 (16-ounce) bottles Italian salad dressing (preferably Wish-Bone)
2 tablespoons Worcestershire sauce
1 tablespoon dry sherry

THE DRILL

1. Score both sides of the steak with a knife in a crisscross pattern, about 1/8-inch deep. Combine the salad dressing, Worcestershire sauce, and sherry in a (one-gallon) zip-top plastic bag, and add the steak. Squeeze out the air and seal the bag; turn to coat the steak. Refrigerate, turning the bag occasionally, at least overnight and up to three days.

2. Oil the grill rack **(but see Rookie Mistake: Greased Lightning on the Rack, p. 83).** Prepare the grill for a medium-hot fire.

3. Remove the steak from the marinade; discard remaining marinade. Place the steak on the rack. Grill until evenly charred, about 10 minutes on each side, and an instant-read thermometer inserted in the center of the steak registers 135°F for medium-rare. Transfer the steak to a cutting board, cover loosely with foil, and let stand about 10 minutes. To serve, slice the steak thinly across the grain.

FLAVORS
2 LBS.
OF STEAK

FOWLER FAMILY STEAK MARINADE

Chris Fowler writes, "For years, my brother Drew and I have used this steak marinade on the grill. It's kind of a hybrid, adapted from different recipes, and as much as I'd like to take the credit, much of it has to go to Drew. (After all, he is a trained chef...)"

THE INGREDIENTS

A few ounces of olive oil (not extra virgin, it has too much olive taste)

The freshly squeezed juice of 2 lemons

3 tablespoons honey

1/2 cup red wine (substitute brandy or Jack Daniel's, or dark beer, if desired)

2 garlic cloves, chopped

1 onion, chopped

1 teaspoon cinnamon, or more to taste

Crushed red pepper flakes (or a tablespoon of Tabasco sauce)

1 teaspoon black pepper

1 teaspoon salt

THE DRILL

1. Combine all the ingredients. Put the steaks in zip-top bags, along with the marinade, at least a day before cooking (two, if possible).

2. Take to the game in the bags, remove and grill.

ALL-STAR BARBECUE DRY RUB

MAKES ABOUT 1 CUP

Use this spice mix to season just about everything.

THE INGREDIENTS

1/4 cup salt
1/4 cup freshly ground black pepper
3 tablespoons garlic powder
2 tablespoons chili powder
2 tablespoons paprika

THE DRILL

In a jar with a tight-fitting lid, combine all the ingredients.

THE HOLY TRINITY OF BARBECUE SAUCES

These three sauces represent a range of flavor profiles favored by some of America's notable barbecue regions. Use them as a binder for a plate of Hickory Stick Pulled Pork Barbecue (p. 94) or as a glaze to apply on grilled foods during the last few minutes over the fire. (Brush them on too soon, and the sugars will char and form a burnt crust.) Make a batch of each, bottle 'em, and let your guests get all saucy.

Eastern North Carolina-Style Barbecue Sauce

Makes about 3 cups

In a large bowl, combine 1 1/2 cups apple cider vinegar, 1 1/2 cups white vinegar, 1 tablespoon sugar, 1 tablespoon salt, 1 tablespoon crushed pepper flakes, 1 tablespoon freshly ground black pepper, and 1 tablespoon hot pepper sauce. (Can be made ahead of time. Store in an airtight container at room temperature for up to two months.)

MAKES
ABOUT
1 CUP

EVERY-DOWN MARINADE

Heavy on the herbs and the bright flavor of lemon, this combo is a chameleon when it comes to marinating usually dull-tasting meats such as boneless, skinless chicken breasts. Use it to add a little extra flavor to anything from vegetables to pork chops or even fish fillets.

THE INGREDIENTS

1/2 cup chopped fresh parsley
1/4 cup chopped fresh basil, cilantro, or oregano
1/4 cup fresh lemon juice
1/2 teaspoon hot pepper sauce
1/2 teaspoon freshly ground black pepper
1/2 teaspoon kosher salt
3 garlic cloves, minced
1/2 to 2/3 cup olive oil

THE DRILL

In a large glass or ceramic bowl, combine the parsley, basil, lemon juice, pepper sauce, ground pepper, salt, and garlic, and beat with a whisk until blended. Gradually add the oil in a slow, steady stream, beating constantly with a whisk until the mixture is blended and slightly thickened.

Tennessee-Style Barbecue Sauce

Makes about 3 1/2 cups

In a small saucepan, combine 1 cup ketchup, 1 (8-ounce) can tomato sauce, 1 cup firmly packed brown sugar, 1 cup apple cider vinegar, 1 tablespoon Worcestershire sauce, 1 tablespoon paprika, 1 1/2 teaspoons onion salt, 1 teaspoon mustard powder, and 1 to 2 teaspoons hot pepper sauce. Cook over medium heat, stirring occasionally, until the brown sugar melts. Reduce the heat and simmer, stirring occasionally, until the flavors are blended, about 10 minutes. (Can be made ahead of time. Cool, transfer to an airtight container, and refrigerate for up to two weeks.)

Kansas City-Style Barbecue Sauce

Makes about 3 1/2 cups

In a small saucepan, combine 2 cups ketchup, 1/2 cup firmly packed dark brown sugar, 1/2 cup butter, 1/2 cup apple cider vinegar, 1/4 cup chili sauce, 1 tablespoon paprika, 2 to 3 teaspoons hot pepper sauce, 1 crushed garlic clove, and 1 teaspoon salt, or to taste. Cook over medium heat, stirring occasionally, until the brown sugar and butter melt and the mixture is well blended. Reduce the heat and simmer, stirring frequently to prevent sticking, about 20 minutes. (Can be made ahead of time. Cool, transfer to an airtight container, and refrigerate for up to two weeks.)

HICKORY STICK PULLED PORK BARBECUE

SERVES 12 TO 15

Want to fix up a batch of long-smoked barbecue without investing in a $10,000 trailer pit? If you're flirting with diehard status and have the better part of a day (or night) to kill down at the stadium, give this hickory-smoked grill method a shot. The smell alone makes this the ideal dish for Hickory Stick game battles between Northwest Missouri and Truman State. After all, the oldest Division II trophy game requires some serious, Division 1 flavors.

THE INGREDIENTS

6 cups hickory chips
1 (5- to 7-pound) Boston-style butt pork roast
Kosher salt, to taste
Freshly ground black pepper, to taste
Hot pepper sauce, to taste
1 cup **Eastern North Carolina-Style** or **Tennessee-Style Barbecue Sauce (pp. 92–3)**, plus additional sauce for serving

THE DRILL

1. One hour before grilling, in a large bowl, soak the hickory chips in enough water to cover, and let the pork stand at room temperature.

2. Prepare the grill for indirect heat **(see Grilling Basics, Play the Zones, p. 80)**.

3. Generously sprinkle salt, ground pepper, and hot pepper sauce over all sides of the pork. Drain one cup of the wood chips, shaking off any excess water. Add the chips to the fire or smoker box, and cover the grill until smoke appears. Oil the grill rack, uncover the grill, and place the rack in the grill. Place the pork on the grill rack over the drip pan. Cover and reduce the heat to low (for a gas grill), or close the vents almost completely (for a charcoal grill). Grill the pork until fork-tender and an instant-read thermometer registers 180°F, four to seven hours, replenishing the briquettes (if using charcoal) and adding the remaining wood chips, one cup at a time, every hour.

MEAT VS. SAUCE
A GAMEDAY GRUDGE MATCH

In the world of tailgating, you've got two types of people: those who insist the most important ingredient in a successful barbecue is the meat, and those who side with the sauce. Think Florida State-Miami, Auburn-Alabama, Texas-Oklahoma. Now think Kirk and Chris. In this debate, the *GameDay* colleagues line up on opposite sides of the ball.

SAUCE!

KIRK HERBSTREIT: "Chris is a rookie when it comes to this. He's more of a highbrow, Manhattan, fine-dining type of guy. I'm a roll-up-the-sleeves-and-have-at-it man. For example, he likes his meat raw—which is just silly. Meat should be cooked 'til it's dry, and it has to be really lean. The sauce is what gives it that juiciness, and you absolutely cannot have too much of a good sauce. He'll say I'm all about the sauce and the meat doesn't matter, but he's just plain wrong. Fact is, you can't have one without the other."

MEAT!

CHRIS FOWLER: "The best sauce in the world can't make up for subpar meat, especially when it's overcooked. Overcooking is the cardinal sin of tailgating. The reason Kirk says the sauce makes the barbecue is because by the time the steak arrives in front of him, it's already been ruined. It's like he's eating a swatch of Bevo's hide. Great sauce is important, and it's nice if it has some zing, but it should complement the meat, not overpower it."

4. Transfer the pork to a cutting board, cover loosely with foil, and let stand 20 minutes. Remove any skin and excess fat from the pork; chop or shred. In a large, disposable foil roasting pan, combine the pork and the barbecue sauce. Serve with additional sauce.

RACK 'EM UP
TACKLING RIBS

Of all the meat products in the tailgate griller's hall of fame, barbecued pork ribs have to be the best *and* the worst of the lot. On the upside, there's the primal joy of diving face-first into a rack o' ribs and scraping the curved bones clean with your hard-working canine teeth. The tender between-bone flesh drips with sauce and juice. And at the end of the feeding frenzy, you're left with a dismantled rib cage and a meat-eating, sauce-smeared smile.

On the downside, there's your biggest enemy, in the words of the old ketchup commercial: anticipation. Cooking good ribs requires a long, slow fire, the better part of a pregame afternoon, and a whole lot of self-control.

Two completely different pork rib cuts — one from the top of the pig, one from the belly — are commonly used, so choose the one that best fits your taste (and pocketbook).

BABY BACK RIBS So-called for their smaller size rather than because of the suckling or non-suckling status of the pig that they came from, baby backs are the bony parts of a pig's loin section and the tidier of the two rib varieties. They're tiny, they're more manageable, and they're pretty damn expensive. If you've got big eaters in your crew, your meat bill will easily outstrip your beer money.

SPARERIBS These meaty wonders — a close neighbor of American bacon — are tasty, heavy, and chockful of flavorful fat. Compared to baby backs, spare-ribs are cheaper and less uniform, but they *do* take longer to cook. If you take the spare route, allow for more time on the grill.

JAYHAWK DOUBLE-CLUTCH PORK RIBS

At his football parties, KU alum and Kansas City native John Heili used to serve a variation of these ribs—meaty, succulent, melt-in-your-mouth wonders that he'd cook on a tiny kettle grill. (He'd make six racks of ribs—enough to qualify as a modern-day version of the loaves and fishes.) The key is to start with a long braise—a wet cooking method that's easily pulled off in your home oven—for tenderness and to finish those suckers off on the grill for a smoky flavor. Perfect for outdoor games when you don't have half a day of grill time.

THE INGREDIENTS

3 pounds pork baby back or spareribs, rinsed and patted dry

For the spice rub:
1 tablespoon packed brown sugar
1 tablespoon paprika
1 teaspoon chili powder
1/4 teaspoon ground red pepper
1/4 teaspoon kosher salt

1/4 cup Dijon mustard
Freshly ground black pepper, to taste
1 cup prepared barbecue sauce (preferably hickory flavor)
2 tablespoons honey

THE DRILL

1. Preheat the oven to 300°F. Place the ribs in the center of an 18 x 24-inch sheet of heavy-duty foil. Bring up the sides of the foil, and double-fold one end to seal. Through the open end, add 1/4 cup of water. Double-fold the remaining foil, leaving enough room for heat to circulate. Transfer the ribs to a large, rimmed baking sheet. Bake until the ribs are tender, about one hour. Cool in the sealed packet for 30 minutes.

2. Meanwhile, oil the grill rack and prepare the grill for a medium-hot fire. To make the spice rub, combine all the ingredients in a cup.

more 👉

3. Carefully open the packet, allowing the steam to escape. Transfer the ribs to another large, rimmed baking sheet; brush both sides with the mustard, then sprinkle with the spice rub and ground black pepper.

4. Place the ribs, meaty side down, on the grill rack. Cover and grill 15 minutes. Turn the ribs and brush with about one-third of the barbecue sauce; cover and grill 10 to 15 minutes. Turn the ribs and repeat. Brush the meaty side of the ribs with the remaining sauce, cover and grill until evenly charred, about five minutes. Drizzle the ribs with the honey and grill, uncovered, just until the honey sets, about five minutes longer.

PLAYMAKER
THE RIB REVERSE

Since a hog's rib cage is all about connective tissue, you'll need to give your ribs plenty of time to cook long and slow—that's what gives perfect ribs their tender texture. (Once the fat and sinews break down, it's all about the meat.)

Unfortunately, that kind of time works against an outdoor tailgater. After all, there are usually burgers and chicken competing for grill space, as well as a million other distractions—like adult beverages to be sipped and opposing fans to taunt. What this calls for is a solid pitchout option.

The best place to start your spice-rubbed racks is in the home kitchen. Bake your ribs in a low oven (about 250°F) for one to two hours the night before gameday to "par cook" (partially cook) them, then refrigerate.

Pack them in a disposable roasting pan and schlep them to the away venue of your choice. The ribs finish cooking on the grill, soaking up a little smoke flavor as they go and benefiting from a liberal, last-minute slathering of sauce.

On the flip side, indoor tailgaters can reverse the whole process. They can start their ribs on the grill for an hour or so over indirect heat, then move them to an oven-proof baking dish with about an inch of barbecue sauce in it. Tent the dish with foil and transfer to a preheated 200°F oven. The ribs will continue to slow-cook for as long as you can keep your hungry crew at bay. The longer they bake, the more they'll melt in your mouth.

G D G

SERVES 12

TOUCHDOWN GRILLED PORK TENDERLOIN

Pure, pristine pig flesh. The pork tenderloin ranks as the leanest, most tender piece of pork available — and as the saying goes, you just can't eat higher on the hog than this. Tenderloin is perfect served warm off the grill but you should take care when cooking this delicate (and pricey) cut, since it's got no fat to baste it from the inside or to protect the delicate meat from fiery flare-ups.

THE INGREDIENTS

3 (1-pound) pork tenderloins
5 tablespoons **All-Star Barbecue Dry Rub (p. 92)** or favorite dry
   rub for ribs
1/2 cup smoky, tomato-based barbecue sauce
1/2 cup ranch salad dressing
1/2 cup hot pepper jelly
2 French baguettes, split
1/2 cup chopped fresh cilantro

THE DRILL

1. Oil the grill rack. Prepare the grill for a medium-hot fire.

2. Pat the pork dry with paper towels. Divide the dry rub and apply evenly over all sides of each tenderloin. In a small saucepan, combine the barbecue sauce and salad dressing. Cook over low heat, stirring occasionally, until hot. Set aside and keep warm.

3. In a small bowl, stir the jelly until smooth and spreadable. Place the pork on the grill rack. Grill, turning occasionally, until browned and an instant-read thermometer inserted into the center of each tenderloin registers 155°F, 15 to 20 minutes, generously brushing each tenderloin with the jelly during the last few minutes of grilling. Transfer the pork to a cutting board; cover loosely with foil and let stand about 10 minutes.

4. Meanwhile, place the baguettes, cut side down, on the grill rack. Grill until lightly toasted. Slice the pork thinly; divide between the bottom halves of the baguettes. Drizzle the pork with some of the sauce, sprinkle with the cilantro, and top with the remaining baguette. Cut each baguette into six sandwiches. Serve with the remaining sauce on the side.

DEEP COVER CHEESE-STUFFED BACON-WRAPPED HOT DOGS

SERVES 8

Bacon. Hot dogs. Processed cheese food. If you're a kid (and you probably still are) it's pretty tough to resist the combination. Cut into one-inch chunks for toothpick-ready portion control or wolf them down by the handful.

THE INGREDIENTS

8 jumbo hot dogs

4 (1-ounce) sticks mild cheddar cheese, each cut lengthwise in half

8 slices good-quality bacon

8 hot dog rolls, split and toasted

Assorted toppings: mustard, ketchup, chili (**such as Lone Star Chili, p. 111**), relish, sauerkraut

THE DRILL

1. Prepare the grill for a medium hot fire.

2. Cut a slit lengthwise along the center of each hot dog, but not all the way through, to create a pocket. Insert a piece of the cheese in each pocket; wrap each hot dog in a slice of bacon.

3. Place the hot dogs on the grill rack. Grill, turning occasionally, until the bacon is crisp, about eight minutes. Place the hot dogs in the rolls and serve with the assorted toppings.

SERVES
8

BRATWURST IN BEER

This Midwestern classic is a staple at any summertime outing, but is particularly associated with tailgates at schools like the University of Wisconsin, Minnesota, and Michigan. A mild sausage made mostly of veal and pork, bratwurst crisps nicely but can dry out quickly if overcooked. A postgrilling beer bath serves to add some aromatic flavors, much-needed moisture, and additional cook time.

THE INGREDIENTS

1/4 cup butter
2 medium onions, sliced into thin rings
4 garlic cloves, finely chopped (optional)
3 to 4 (12-ounce) cans cheap beer (Wisconsin fans insist on
    Pabst Blue Ribbon)
8 bratwurst links
8 small, crusty hoagie rolls
Whole-grain mustard
Dill pickle spears

THE DRILL

1. Prepare the grill for a medium-hot fire.

2. Place the butter in a medium disposable foil roasting pan. Place the pan on the grill rack and cook until the butter melts. Add the onions and garlic (if using); cook until softened, three to five minutes. Add the beer and bring to a simmer. Place the pan on the low heat zone and keep the onion mixture warm.

3. Place the bratwurst on the grill rack. Grill, turning occasionally, until evenly charred, four to five minutes. Transfer the bratwurst to the onion mixture and let stand until ready to serve.

4. With tongs, place the bratwurst in the rolls. Serve with the onions, mustard, and pickle spears.

SAUSAGE
THE BEST OF THE WURST

In the days of yore, when dinosaurs roamed the earth and Joe Paterno was starting out in high school, there were only two kinds of sausage allowed on a tailgate grill—bratwurst in the upper Midwest and hot dogs everywhere else. But despite its somewhat down-market nutritional reputation, sausage has made a comeback in recent years as upscale grocery stores and boutique butchers have begun experimenting with different ways to cater to health-conscious patrons. (Read: the chicken and turkey crowd.)

The sausage section of any supermarket is packed with options for a simple but versatile gameday menu. Pick up a few different kinds (spicy beef, fancy poultry, savory lamb, old-school brats) and your work as cook/host is reduced significantly. Just open the packages, grill, and try not to get the different types mixed up.

Though local butchers may make their own special sausages, here's a basic guide to varieties that are readily available nationwide. Buy a few packs and mix 'em up.

SMOKED SAUSAGE

Usually made of beef or pork, smoked sausage is a catch-all category in which you can find flavors ranging from garlicky Polish kielbasa to pepper-heavy Louisiana links. Since the smoking process essentially cooks this variety, they don't require a lot of grill time. These sausages tend to be relatively high in fat—though you'll find that the fat content varies depending on the producer—which makes them a favorite of indulgent omnivores everywhere.

On the Grill: Smoked sausages brown up nicely, but often burst when the internal juices turn to steam. When that happens, juices and potentially flammable grease will hit the fire, so watch out for flare-ups.

On the Plate: Serve on a crusty roll with a whole-grain or Creole mustard.

THE CLASSIC HOT DOG

Though frankfurters are often relegated to "kids' food" status, a good hot dog delivers a burst of meaty flavor, a rush of salt, and just the right amount of crunch. Even for adults, there are powerful memories (ballparks, campfire dining) in every crisp-skinned dog. Since the cheaper varieties often use a lot of artificial coloring and fillers, we splurge on all-beef Hebrew Nationals.

On the Grill: Like a bald man on a sunny beach, watch for a quick burn. Standard-size hot dogs are precooked, and require only a few minutes of grill time to plump up and brown to perfection. A few seconds too long and you'll be picking soot off your dog.

On the Plate: Simple is best. Squishy white buns toasted a bit on the grill, then slathered with yellow mustard and sauerkraut.

LOUISIANA HOT LINKS

A smooth-textured pork or beef sausage with plenty of sweat-inducing afterburn, this red-tinged specialty has a distinctive, tangy flavor and more than its share of ground red pepper and paprika. Take ample time between bites — the spice can sneak up on your taste buds. (So have a beer handy, just in case.)

On the Grill: Being fresh and chock full of fat, the hot link requires special attention during cooking. Expect a fair amount of sputtering grease and use a fork to poke holes in the skin halfway through. Move to the low heat zone if flare-ups become a problem.

On the Plate: Slice a soft French loaf in sections and dress it like a po' boy — with cooling mayo, whole-grain Creole mustard, shredded lettuce, and chopped ripe tomato.

CHICKEN SAUSAGE

A relatively new appearance on the scene, these sausages have broad appeal with the "all white meat" crowd. Boutique butchers mix up batches of more traditional varieties (andouille, Italian sausage) with new-school flavor combinations (cilantro and bell pepper, garlic and basil with sun-dried tomato chunks). At home or away, take the same precautions that you would with other types of uncooked chicken—keep well chilled until just before grilling and wash your hands after handling to prevent bacterial cross-contamination of other foods.

On the Grill: Chicken sausages require longer grilling to cook thoroughly, so ask your butcher about approximate times as he wraps your order. (Ours gave a ballpark of 25 minutes over medium heat.) Start them on the low heat zone, then finish over higher heat until the skin browns and turns crispy.

On the Plate: A well-cooked chicken sausage can be on the dry side, so split it down the middle and then open the link onto a toasted pita bread that's been spread with flavored mayonnaise and peppery micro-greens.

SOY "VEGGIE DOGS"

Low-fat, high-protein "soysages" provide an eat-along alternative for meatless diners. Some have the added "advantage" of being fat-free, and, so, not too surprisingly, these "tofu tubes" don't faithfully reproduce the trademark flavors of their carne-compliant cousins. But they are efficient condiment-delivery devices that fit nicely on a standard hot dog bun.

On the Grill: Since soy dogs don't have proper casings, they cook quickly and tend to blister over direct heat. Grill them on the low heat zone.

On the Plate: Serve on a split and toasted multigrain roll with Dijon mustard and crispy salad greens.

UNION BAY SALMON

SERVES 4

The practice of nautical "stern-gating" on Union Bay off of Lake Washington is a tradition at the University of Washington in Seattle. At Husky Stadium, fans show up in boats and moor within sight of the stadium. Before the game, they wave down a shuttle boat and head for their seats. Pacific salmon is a regional taste treat in the Northwest; this grilled variation uses a spice rub and saucy glaze for extra flavor.

THE INGREDIENTS

4 (6-ounce) center-cut skinned salmon fillets
1 tablespoon Cajun-style fish and seafood seasoning
1/2 cup **Kansas City-Style Barbecue Sauce (p. 93)** or your
favorite tomato-based barbecue sauce

THE DRILL

1. Oil the grill rack. Prepare the grill for a medium-hot fire.

2. Spray both sides of the salmon with nonstick cooking spray. Spread the seasoning on a plate. Place each piece of salmon, skinned side up, in the seasoning to coat.

3. Place the salmon, seasoned side down, on the grill rack. Grill until the seasoning forms a crust, about five minutes. Turn the salmon and brush evenly with the sauce. Cover and grill until just opaque in the center, four to five minutes longer. Serve at once.

SERVES 4

FISH·IN·THE·POCKET

This variation on the classic *en papillote* method of cooking fish makes for a great do-ahead alternative at any tailgate. Spend a little kitchen time setting up your packets and bring them to the game in an ice chest (double-bagged to prevent leakage).

THE INGREDIENTS

3 tablespoons unsalted butter, softened
4 scallions, thinly sliced
Freshly ground white pepper, to taste
8 thin lemon slices
2 medium shallots, thinly sliced
2 tablespoons chopped fresh flat-leaf parsley
2 tablespoons chopped fresh dill
4 (6-ounce) skinned flounder, snapper, catfish, or salmon fillets

THE DRILL

1. Prepare the grill for a medium-hot fire.

2. Spread the center of four (12 x 16-inch) sheets of heavy-duty foil with two tablespoons of the butter. In a medium skillet, melt the remaining one tablespoon of butter over medium-high heat. Add the scallions and white pepper; cook, stirring occasionally, until softened, about three minutes.

3. To make the packets, place one fillet in the center of each sheet of foil. Layer the top of each fillet with two lemon slices and one-quarter each of the scallions, shallots, parsley, and dill. Turn up the edges of the foil; double fold the edges to make a tight seal.

4. Place the packets on the grill rack. Grill until the fillets are just opaque in the center, 10 to 12 minutes. (Open the packets carefully when testing for doneness, as steam will escape.)

THE PURSUIT OF FRESH FISH

The first rule of seafood is to always buy fresh—preferably within a day of when you intend to cook it. It's the only real way you avoid the heartbreak of S.F.S.—Stinky Fish Syndrome. (And be honest: No tailgater wants to face the dread fish funk.)

The best thing to do is to hit the grocery store and chat up the fish guy on Friday night. Ask him about the freshest fish and have him wrap up a few fillets. Tell him you're cooking these in a packet and ask him for approximate cooking times. As a rule, fish guys love to talk and can even suggest complimentary herbs or other tips for making your finfish more flavorful—fresh herbs, thin slices of lemon or lime, etc.

CHAPTER 6 ☞
SLO-MO

LONG-COOKING, BIG-BATCH GUT-WARMERS

CHALK TALK

In a world of instant soup, microwave dinners, and drive-thru dining, there's really no substitute for taking your time — slowing down and cooking a hearty dish that might well garner you tailgate celebrity among your fellow fans. The truth is that anyone can go for the easy score. Ever wonder why there are so many bowls of chips and salsa at a rookie tailgate?

When most of us think about slow cooking, we conjure Halloween images of witches around a steaming cauldron ("Bubble, bubble, toil and trouble ... "). But, the truth is that the more time-consuming cooking methods — stewing, smothering, braising, and souping (if that's a real word) — are pretty low-maintenance once you get the hang of them.

These slow-cooked hot dishes are perfectly suited for indoor tailgates but can also save the day when an outdoor party is spoiled by a few snow flurries or raindrops. Cooking most of these recipes on-site requires specialized equipment, such as high-pressure propane burners and the appropriate safety equipment. It's perhaps better to spend a midweek evening cooking up a batch of your favorite chili, either with beans, like

Fred's Famous Tar Heel Chili (p. 112), or without, like **Lone Star Chili (opposite)**. You can also prepare a robust pot of our **Ivy League Clam Chowder (p. 120)**, then truck it out to the stadium come the weekend.

The time and care that go into these dishes will set you apart from the microwave and drive-thru crowd. Push aside the salsa bowls, and let your admiring friends dig in to your hearty, slow-cooked concoctions.

Give these dishes a try — just and give 'em plenty of time to get good. You'll be amply rewarded once the party gets rolling.

SERVES
6

LONE STAR CHILI

Before there was chips and salsa, before there were breakfast burritos, there was chili con carne (chili with meat). This simple stew of beef and hot peppers takes a 20-minute pregame session (chopping and browning, mostly), then simmers quietly on the back burner until halftime. It's spicy, gut-warming, beer-friendly, and the perfect one-pot meal for any all-guy gathering. And besides having a remarkably high payoff-to-effort ratio, once you make this simple dish a few times, you've pretty much mastered it. Make it chunky style for by-the-bowl feasting, or break up the meaty clusters and it's a damn fine hot dog topper.

THE INGREDIENTS

2 pounds lean ground beef (the leaner the better)
3 tablespoons olive oil
2 large onions, chopped
3 garlic cloves, minced
5 tablespoons chili powder
1 1/2 tablespoons ground cumin
2 teaspoons dried oregano, crushed
1 teaspoon freshly ground black pepper
1/2 teaspoon ground red pepper
3 cups hot water
1/2 (6-ounce) can tomato paste

THE DRILL

1. Set a large, heavy pot over medium heat. Add the beef and cook, breaking it up with a spoon, until brown. Transfer the beef to a bowl and set aside. Discard any drippings in the pot.

2. Heat the oil in the same pot over medium-high heat. Add the onions and garlic: cook until softened, about five minutes. Add the chili powder, cumin, oregano, black and red pepper and cook, stirring constantly, just until fragrant. Stir in the reserved beef, hot water, and tomato paste, and bring to a boil. Reduce the heat and simmer until the mixture is thick and the flavors are blended, at least 30 minutes longer.

FRED'S FAMOUS TAR HEEL CHILI

SERVES
20

Fred Thompson, the kitchen wizard behind this project, wanted to make sure to include a recipe for all the bean-loving chili fans out there. His time-tested recipe has seen its fair share of Tar Heel games and Appalachian State University parking lots.

THE INGREDIENTS

1 (1-pound) bag dried pinto beans, picked over and rinsed
2 1/2 pounds ground beef chuck
2 pounds ground pork
3 large bell peppers of assorted colors, chopped
2 large onions, chopped
1/2 cup chili powder
2 tablespoons cumin seeds
1 teaspoon dried oregano
1 (28-ounce) can + 1 (14 1/2-ounce) can diced tomatoes, with their juice
1/2 cup fresh parsley leaves, chopped
Salt and freshly ground pepper, to taste
Chopped onion, shredded cheddar cheese, sour cream, and salsa, for garnish

THE DRILL

1. Soak the dried beans according to the package directions and drain. In a pot, combine the beans with enough water to cover by two inches. Bring just to a boil. Reduce the heat and simmer the beans until almost tender, about an hour.

2. Set an eight-quart Dutch oven over medium-high heat. In batches, add the beef and pork. Cook, breaking the meat up with a spoon, until well browned (don't crowd the pot or the meat will steam, not brown). Transfer each batch to a bowl using a slotted spoon.

3. Heat the drippings in the same pot over medium heat. Add the bell peppers, onions, chili powder, cumin seeds, and oregano; cook, stirring occasionally, until the vegetables are softened, about 15 minutes. Add the tomatoes with their juice and the reserved meat, and simmer for one hour. Add the beans and simmer until the chili is thickened and the beans are tender, about an hour longer. Stir in the parsley, salt, and pepper. Garnish each serving with onion, cheese, sour cream, and salsa.

AUDIBLE
A QUICK COUNT

For a speedier chili, instead of dried beans, use two (16-ounce) cans of pinto, kidney, or black beans, rinsed and drained. Prepare the recipe as directed, except omit Step 1 and after adding the beans in Step 3, reduce the cooking time to 30 minutes.

CHILI FACE-OFF
TO BEAN OR NOT TO BEAN?

At the risk of stumbling into a culinary religious war, we're including two chili recipes— one for each side of the beans/ no beans rivalry. A certain amount of conflict is to be expected at a football game, especially when there's chili involved, but we really don't want to complicate things by choosing sides here.

So the basic Lone Star Chili (p. 111) takes care of our readers from College Station, Austin, El Paso, Lubbock, and San Antonio. Fred's Famous Tar Heel Chili (these pages) uses pinto beans and should satisfy aficionados of frijoles just about everywhere else. If you really don't give a damn, then they're both good for just about any indoor game-viewing party.

As the diplomatic Fred Thompson (of Fred's Famous Tar Heel Chili) puts it, "There are certain things that have to be acceptable to Texans."

COOKING OVERTIME CROCK-POT ROAST BEEF

SERVES 12

Here's a tender, meaty treat from your friend the Crock-Pot. This slow-cooked pot roast is a snap to make, and you can leave it cooking overnight. The shreds of beef float in a flavorful gravy, providing this dish's action-packed flavor. The Cooking Overtime Crock-Pot Roast Beef also lends itself to variations: Put it on a loaf of French bread with mayo, lettuce, tomato, and pickle slices for a serviceable New Orleans po'boy, or slather it with **Blue Devil Cheese and Bacon Dip (p. 48)**, for a shot of tangy pork goodness.

THE INGREDIENTS

3 cups water

2 teaspoons garlic powder

2 teaspoons dried oregano

1 teaspoon salt

1 teaspoon freshly ground pepper

1 teaspoon dried basil

1 teaspoon onion salt

1 teaspoon dried parsley

1 (0.7-ounce) envelope Italian salad dressing and recipe mix

1 bay leaf

1 (5-pound) beef eye-round roast

2 loaves crusty Italian bread, split

1 tablespoon olive oil

2 medium onions, sliced

1 (16-ounce) jar roasted red peppers, drained and sliced

1 (12-ounce) jar sliced banana peppers, drained

THE DRILL

1. In a medium saucepan, combine the water, garlic powder, oregano, salt, ground pepper, basil, onion salt, parsley, dressing and recipe mix, and bay leaf. Mix well and bring to a boil.

2. Place the beef in a six-quart slow-cooker. Pour the mixture over the beef. Cover and cook until the beef is fork-tender, four to five hours on high or 10 to 12 hours on low.

3. Meanwhile, in a large skillet, heat the oil over medium-high heat. Add the onions and cook, stirring occasionally, until golden, about 10 minutes. Set aside.

4. Transfer the beef to a cutting board and discard the bay leaf. With two forks, shred the beef into small pieces. Transfer to a bowl, and stir in enough of the cooking liquid to moisten.

5. Place the beef on the bottom halves of the loaves. Drizzle the beef with some of the cooking liquid. Top each half with the reserved onion, the roasted peppers, banana peppers, and remaining bread. Cut each loaf crosswise into six sandwiches.

PLAYMAKER

THE TIME'S-RUNNING-OUT, SKIM-AND-SLURP METHOD

In many slow-cooked dishes, flavors and textures can change over time, so it's always good to take a cue from professional chefs and make sure to taste your masterwork before sticking in a ladle and calling it dinner.

Since many of the recipes in this chapter call for frying onions, they also contain an extra bit of fat to help you avoid burning the goods (and when you're sweating an onion, it's always better to have too much grease than too little). About 20 minutes before serving, let your dish simmer, and see how much grease pools up on the surface of the pot. If it seems like a bit much, carefully skim it off into a disposable cup. Then take a couple of plastic spoons and check the flavor balance. Does it need salt? Could it use a little more chili powder? If so, add a bit of whatever your mouth tells you is missing, give it a stir, and taste until you get it right. Why two spoons? No double-dipping, cowboy. You've got *guests*, y'know.

FIGHTING IRISH BEEF STEW

SERVES 4 TO 6

Irish stew on a cold winter's afternoon: You just flat out ain't gonna get any better than that on a frigid gameday in South Bend, Indiana, or anywhere else. This is a slow-cooked classic that takes particularly well to the "chill overnight and reheat" treatment.

THE INGREDIENTS

2 tablespoons olive oil
1 1/4 pounds boneless top round or chuck steak, cut into one-inch pieces
6 large garlic cloves, minced
6 cups reduced-sodium beef broth or homemade beef stock
1 cup Guinness Draught
1 cup fruity red wine
2 tablespoons tomato paste
1 tablespoon sugar
1 tablespoon dried thyme
1 tablespoon Worcestershire sauce
2 bay leaves
2 tablespoons butter
3 pounds baking potatoes, peeled and cut into 1/2-inch cubes
2 cups carrots, cut into 1/4-inch-thick slices
1 large onion, chopped
Salt and freshly ground pepper, to taste
2 tablespoons chopped fresh parsley

THE DRILL

1. In a large Dutch oven, heat the oil over medium-high heat. Add the beef and cook, stirring occasionally, until browned on all sides, about five minutes. Add the garlic and cook, stirring constantly, until fragrant, about a minute. Stir in the broth, Guinness, wine, tomato paste, sugar, thyme, Worcestershire sauce, and bay leaves, and bring to a boil. Reduce the heat and simmer, covered, stirring occasionally, for one hour.

2. Meanwhile, in a large saucepan, melt the butter over medium heat. Add the potatoes, carrots, and onion and cook, stirring occasionally, until the vegetables are golden, about 20 minutes.

3. Add the vegetables to the beef mixture. Simmer, uncovered, until the beef and vegetables are very tender, about 40 minutes. Discard the bay leaves, skim off any fat from the surface, and stir in the salt and pepper. (Can be made ahead of time. Cool, transfer to an airtight container, and refrigerate for up to two days.) Sprinkle with parsley before serving.

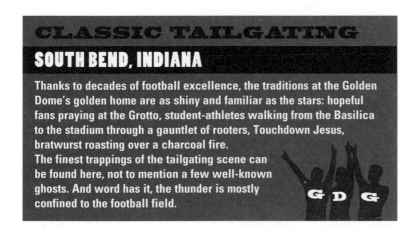

CLASSIC TAILGATING

SOUTH BEND, INDIANA

Thanks to decades of football excellence, the traditions at the Golden Dome's golden home are as shiny and familiar as the stars: hopeful fans praying at the Grotto, student-athletes walking from the Basilica to the stadium through a gauntlet of rooters, Touchdown Jesus, bratwurst roasting over a charcoal fire.
The finest trappings of the tailgating scene can be found here, not to mention a few well-known ghosts. And word has it, the thunder is mostly confined to the football field.

HUDDLE-UP ONION SOUP

SERVES 4

This is a combination of a basic onion soup (veg alert: This recipe contains beef stock) topped with a slab of savory cheese toast. The floating bread softens as you eat while simultaneously thickening the soup, much like when you crumble crackers into a bowl of chili. This recipe is also a chance to expand your cheese vocabulary beyond the deli-counter trifecta of cheddar, Swiss, and American.

THE INGREDIENTS

8 slices (1/4-inch-thick) French baguette
I garlic clove, unpeeled
2 tablespoons canola oil
2 medium Spanish onions, thinly sliced
I teaspoon sugar
1/4 cup dry sherry
2 (10 1/2-ounce) cans condensed French onion soup
2 cups water
I (10 1/2-ounce) can condensed beef consommé
1/2 teaspoon dried thyme
1/2 teaspoon garlic powder
I tablespoon sherry vinegar
Kosher salt and freshly ground pepper, to taste
4 slices Swiss cheese
4 slices provolone cheese
4 tablespoons freshly grated Parmesan cheese

THE DRILL

I. To make the croutons, preheat the oven to 325°F. Place the baguette slices in a single layer on a baking sheet and bake until crisp, about five minutes. Meanwhile, cut off the tip from the narrow end of the garlic clove. Rub both sides of the baguette slices with the exposed tip of the garlic and set aside.

2. In a large Dutch oven, heat the oil over medium heat. Add the onions and sugar and cook, stirring occasionally, until the onions are dark amber brown and very tender, 25 to 30 minutes. Add the sherry and cook, stirring to scrape any browned bits from the bottom of the pot, for about five minutes. Stir in the soup, water, consommé, thyme, and garlic powder and bring to a boil. Reduce the heat and simmer until the flavors are blended, about 20 minutes. Stir in the vinegar, salt, and pepper. (Can be made ahead of time. Cool, transfer to an airtight container, and refrigerate for up to three days. Return to a boil before proceeding to Step 3.)

3. Preheat the broiler. Place four one-cup ovenproof soup bowls on a baking sheet. Ladle the soup evenly among the bowls. Layer the top of each serving with two of the croutons, one slice of the Swiss, one slice of the provolone, and one tablespoon of the Parmesan. Broil four inches from heat until the cheeses are bubbly and golden, about five minutes.

IVY LEAGUE CLAM CHOWDER

SERVES 6 TO 8

New Englanders, did you think we would forget about you? Cold weather games in the Northeast are all about the chowder, and this easy version packs a *wicked smart* punch into your gameday thermos. How can you go wrong with thick bacon and heavy cream? Convenient canned clams make it easy for beginners to learn the style while avoiding clam shell shock. A nod of the helmet to every *chowdahead* in the house ...

CLASSIC TAIL-GATING

NEW HAVEN, CONNECTICUT

For some time now, despite evidence to the contrary, Yalies have laid claim to inventing the tailgate back in 1904. No matter. It's something of a thrill to see such advocates of tradition at work (especially for the Yale-Harvard game). Raccoon coats, monogrammed flasks, wicker picnic baskets, candelabras, quail's eggs, and milk punch (without the milk). Not to worry: Out on the field, they've happily embraced the forward pass.

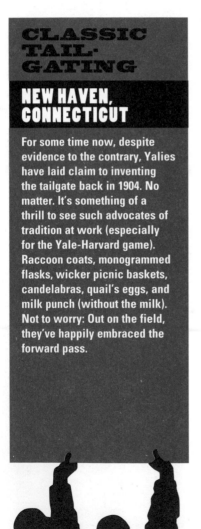

THE INGREDIENTS

1 teaspoon vegetable oil
1/4 pound sliced applewood or other smoked bacon, diced
1 large onion, chopped
2 large white potatoes, peeled and diced
3 cups heavy or whipping cream
1 (8-ounce) bottle clam juice
1 cup water
4 (6 1/2-ounce) cans chopped clams (do not drain)
Kosher salt and freshly ground pepper, to taste
Chopped fresh chives
Oyster crackers

THE DRILL

1. In a four- to six-quart saucepot, heat the oil over medium heat. Add the bacon and cook, stirring occasionally, until crisp. Add the onion and cook until softened, five to eight minutes. Add the potatoes and cook, stirring occasionally, about three minutes. Add the cream, clam juice, and water; bring to a boil. Reduce the heat and simmer until the potatoes are tender, about 25 minutes.

2. Stir in the clams with their liquid; simmer until heated through, about five minutes longer. Stir in the salt and pepper, ladle the chowder into bowls, and sprinkle with chives. Serve with oyster crackers.

SERVES 8 TO 10

BOWL DAY CHOWDER

Legend in the Deep South has it that eating black-eyed peas and stewed collard greens on New Year's Day is supposed to provide luck and money. This take on the traditional Southern favorite Hoppin' John (black-eyed peas and rice) lets you double your good fortune in a single serving—all while providing minimum distraction from a solid day of bowl games.

THE INGREDIENTS

4 cups dried black-eyed peas, picked over and rinsed
2 tablespoons unsalted butter
2 medium onions, diced
4 celery stalks, diced
2 leeks, trimmed to white parts only, cleaned, and chopped
2 large carrots, chopped
1 red bell pepper, diced
1 green bell pepper, diced
1 jalapeño chili, seeded and minced (optional)
4 garlic cloves, peeled
2 sprigs fresh thyme
1 bay leaf
1 (48-ounce) can reduced-sodium chicken broth or 6 cups
    homemade chicken stock
1 smoked ham hock
2 tomatoes, chopped
1 tablespoon balsamic vinegar
1 (16-ounce) bag frozen, chopped collard greens
1 cup diced smoked ham
Salt and freshly ground pepper, to taste
Cooked white rice (optional)

THE DRILL

1. Soak the dried peas according to package directions; drain.

2. Melt the butter in a large Dutch oven over medium heat. Add the onions, celery, leeks, carrots, bell peppers, and jalapeño (if using); cook,

more

RED-SHIRTING

FLAVORS IMPROVE WITH TIME

Even though it might seem a bit counterintuitive, there are times when it's best to prepare a slow-cooked dish the day or night *before* you intend to eat it. Interestingly enough, the same goes for chili, gumbo, and Cajun red beans.

The principle involves a fluid combination of flavors—the longer the various components of a braise, stew, or soup hang around together, the better. Spices infuse vegetables, meaty chunks absorb stock or gravy, and textures smooth themselves out. Old-school cooks call this "letting the flavors marry." If that sounds a bit drastic, think of it more as letting the tastes live together for a while. (Nothing permanent, you understand, just a little while to see how it all works out.)

For morning or early after-noon kickoffs, this basic bit of kitchen physics plays to your advantage. Cook your chili on Thursday night, then chill it safely in your fridge. Then you can sleep in on Saturday, reheat your slow-cooked masterpiece, and show up at the stadium (or your pal's living room) unhurried and ready to cheer.

stirring occasionally, until the vegetables have softened but have not browned. Transfer to a bowl and set aside.

3. Place the garlic, thyme sprigs, and bay leaf in a triple-thick piece of cheesecloth (or tea infuser); tie with kitchen string to form a package. In the same pot, combine the broth, ham hock, herb package, and the reserved vegetables; bring to a boil. Reduce the heat and simmer, covered, 15 minutes. Stir in the dried peas and return to a boil. Reduce the heat and simmer until the peas are tender, about an hour.

4. Meanwhile, in a medium bowl, combine the tomatoes and vinegar. Transfer the ham hock to a cutting board and cool. Remove the meat from the hock and chop; discard the bone.

5. Add the collard greens to the peas and cook, stirring occasionally, until the collards are heated through, about 10 minutes. Add the reserved meat from the hock, the ham, salt, and pepper; cook until heated through. Top with the tomato mixture and serve over rice (if using).

SERVES 16

SHREDDED D PORK

What's better than having strips of tender pork shoulder mounted on a sandwich roll and topped with crunchy, tangy coleslaw? Well, not having to tend a smoldering wood fire all night to get it, for one. While Carolina barbecue fans might turn their noses up at this easy, make-at-home version, it's a good approximation of the regional style, and though it lacks the hickory-smoked punch of the real McCoy, it's a lot more adaptable.

THE INGREDIENTS

3 to 4 tablespoons **All-Star Barbecue Dry Rub (p. 92)** or
 favorite dry rub for ribs
I (5- to 7-pound) Boston-style shoulder butt pork roast
2 (18-ounce) bottles prepared barbecue sauce
1/2 cup apple-cider vinegar
3 garlic cloves, peeled and crushed
2 dashes Liquid Smoke
Water
16 white hamburger buns, split
Extra barbeque sauce and **Kickback Coleslaw (p. 160)**

THE DRILL

I. Apply the dry rub all over the pork; let marinate at room temperature for 30 minutes.

2. Meanwhile, place the barbecue sauce, vinegar, garlic, and Liquid Smoke in a six-quart slow-cooker. Fill one empty bottle of the barbecue sauce with water; add to the sauce mixture and stir to blend. Add the pork. Cover and cook until the pork is fork-tender, four to five hours on high or 10 to 12 hours on low.

3. Transfer the pork to a cutting board. With two forks, shred the pork into small pieces; transfer to a bowl and stir in enough of the cooking liquid to moisten. (You can also use the cooking liquid as a sauce when assembling the sandwiches.)

4. Fill the hamburger buns with the pulled pork; top with extra barbecue sauce and coleslaw.

EXTRA POINT

Refrigerate any leftovers in an airtight container for up to a week or freeze for up to four months.

SMOKIN' CHIPOTLE PORK STEW

SERVES 4

Here we have a deliciously thick stew that comes off like a cross between chili con carne and a double-cut pork chop, making this a tastier alternative to the standard tailgate "bowl of red." The chipotle chili peppers give the dish a pleasantly smoky flavor with plenty of fiery aftertaste. It might take a few batches of this dish to dial in the heat levels, so test it first on your most macho chili-head buddies. Heck, they'll eat anything ...

THE INGREDIENTS

2 tablespoons olive or vegetable oil

1 1/2 pounds boneless pork shoulder, cut into one-inch cubes

2 medium onions, diced

1 (12-ounce) bottle or can beer

5 to 7 chipotle peppers in adobo sauce ✚ 3 tablespoons adobo sauce

2 teaspoons ground cumin, or to taste

Salt and freshly ground pepper, to taste

CHIPOTLE PEPPERS
SMOKEY, SAUCY, AND SATISFYING

Canned chipotles in adobo sauce are the perfect ingredient for adding that classic combination of spice and smoke to a variety of dishes. The chilis themselves are smoked jalapeños, not over-whelmingly spicy but hot enough to serve your mouth a nice dollop of warmth. They're packed with a tomato sauce that soaks up a lot of the ambient flavors, and you can even use the sauce as a great ingredient by itself.

Until you get a feel for how much heat these babies can add to a dish, go easy on them. The heat can sneak up on you, so make sure you adapt your final heat level to the crowd rather than the party's resident fire-breathers.

Chipotles are also kind of a mess to work with, especially after they've been soaking in the sauce. You can control some of the heat, but still keep the smoky flavor, by cutting the chilis

open on a cutting board and removing the seeds and the light-colored membrane from inside. These membranes are the plant parts that deliver capsaicin, the chemical that causes the after burn.

G D G

THE DRILL

1. Heat a large Dutch oven over medium-high heat until very hot, about two minutes. Add the oil. Add the pork and cook, in batches if necessary, until browned on all sides. Transfer the pork to a bowl and set aside.

2. Reduce the heat to low. Add the onions, stirring to scrape up the browned bits from the bottom of the pot. Cover with a tight-fitting lid and cook, stirring occasionally, until the onions are golden and slightly browned around the edges, about 10 minutes. Add the reserved pork, beer, chipotles, adobo sauce, cumin, salt, and pepper; stir until combined. Simmer, covered, stirring occasionally, until the pork is fork-tender, about 1 1/2 hours.

TIP
Serve this dish as a stew or transfer the pork to a cutting board. With two forks, shred the chunks into small pieces and use as a filling for tacos or sandwiches.

IN THE RED ZONE SAUCE (BASIC MARINARA)

MAKES ABOUT 14 CUPS

This is a great all-purpose pasta sauce (see **No-Hassle Baked Ziti, p. 149**). Sure, you can buy a million different brands of spaghetti sauce at your local supermarket. This version is made from scratch and isn't much more challenging than opening a jar. But this might be the best "first dish" for any rookie cook because it's easy to make and has countless variations. Master the recipe, then add browned Italian sausage, and follow that by learning to make your Nonna Julia's meatballs or by trying an all-vegetarian marinara for date night. Make a bunch and freeze half the sauce in one- or two-cup airtight containers up to six months if you like.

THE INGREDIENTS

2 (28-ounce) cans whole peeled tomatoes with their liquid

2 (28-ounce) cans crushed tomatoes

2 tablespoons dried basil

1 tablespoon sugar

1 tablespoon dried oregano

2 tablespoons dried basil

1 tablespoon garlic powder

2 teaspoons onion powder

Salt and freshly ground pepper, to taste

THE DRILL

In a five-quart Dutch oven, combine all the ingredients and bring to a boil over medium heat. Reduce the heat and simmer, stirring about every 15 minutes, until the sauce has thickened slightly and the flavors are blended, about 1 1/2 hours.

SERVES 4 TO 6

FIRST-STRING ITALIAN SAUSAGE PASTA

When people think of Italian sausages, they often have in mind a gargantuan sandwich of the sort found at street fairs: full to bursting with plump, grilled links that come smothered in caramelized onions and strips of green bell pepper. In this incarnation, we take those vibrant flavors, add a little tomato, and adapt this classic to a tailgating pasta bowl.

THE INGREDIENTS

2 tablespoons olive oil
1 pound sweet or hot Italian sausage links, casings removed
1 medium onion, cut into very thin rings
1 green bell pepper, cut into thin strips
4 garlic cloves, minced
1 (14 1/2-ounce) can diced tomatoes with their juice
1 (6-ounce) can tomato paste
Salt and freshly ground pepper, to taste
1 (1-pound) box medium pasta, such as penne or mostaccioli,
    cooked according to package directions

THE DRILL

1. In a large skillet, heat one tablespoon of the oil over medium-high heat. Add the sausage and cook, breaking it up into pieces, until well browned. Transfer the sausage with a slotted spoon to a bowl.

2. Heat the remaining tablespoon of oil with the drippings in the same skillet. Add the onion and cook, stirring to scrape up any browned bits from the bottom of the skillet, until softened. Add the bell pepper and cook until softened, about five minutes. Add the reserved sausage and garlic; cook, stirring frequently, about three minutes. Stir in the tomatoes with their juice and the tomato paste. Reduce the heat and simmer until the sauce is thickened, 25 to 30 minutes. Toss the sauce with the pasta and serve at once.

EXTRA POINTS

For a distinctly Mediterranean Sloppy Joe, prepare the recipe as directed, except omit the pasta and diced tomatoes. Reduce the amount of tomato paste to 1/2 of the 6-ounce can and add to the sausage mixture in Step 3 along with a 3/4 cup of beer. Serve as a sandwich filling with French bread or toasted hard rolls.

127

SOUTH LOUISIANA RED BEANS

SERVES 8

This slow-cooked wonder is a Monday lunch staple in New Orleans kitchens, but it works just as well on gameday as a one-pot substitute for a chili-jaded crowd. Start with canned beans and you can cut the cooking time significantly. You can always omit the sausage for a hearty, vegetarian-friendly entrée.

THE INGREDIENTS

4 tablespoons vegetable oil
1 pound andouille, kielbasa, or smoked sausage, sliced 1/4-inch thick
2 (15-ounce) cans red kidney beans, drained and rinsed
1 large onion, diced fine
4 garlic cloves, minced
2 celery stalks, diced fine
1 large green bell pepper, chopped
1/2 to 1 cup beer

Herb and spice mix:
2 teaspoons dried basil
2 teaspoons salt
1 teaspoon freshly ground pepper
3/4 teaspoon dried rubbed sage
1/2 teaspoon ground white pepper
1/4 teaspoon ground red pepper

2 bay leaves
1 bunch scallions, chopped
1/4 cup chopped fresh parsley
Cooked white rice

THE DRILL

1. In a large Dutch oven, heat two tablespoons of the oil over medium heat. Add the sausage and cook, stirring occasionally, until lightly browned. Transfer the sausage to a plate and set aside.

2. Heat the remaining two tablespoons of oil in the same pot over medium heat. Add the onion and garlic; cook, stirring occasionally, until the onion is softened. Add the celery and bell pepper; cook, stirring occasionally, until softened, about five minutes. Stir in the beans and 1/2 cup of the beer; cook until the mixture is slightly soupy, about five minutes, adding the remaining 1/2 cup of beer if necessary.

3. Meanwhile, in a cup, combine all the ingredients for the herb and spice mix.

4. Stir in the bay leaves and enough of the spice mix to taste. Reduce the heat and simmer, stirring occasionally, until the flavors are well integrated, at least 45 minutes.

5. About 20 minutes before serving, transfer one cup of bean mixture to a bowl and mash with a fork. Stir the mashed beans into the remaining beans. (The starch from the mashed beans will add a silky texture to the dish.) Stir in the scallions and parsley; simmer about five minutes longer. Season with additional spice mix, if desired. Serve over rice.

BAYOU CLASSIC CHICKEN AND SAUSAGE GUMBO

SERVES 6

This classic Louisiana concoction is versatile, popular, and good on any cold day (or what Bayou State locals call "gumbo weather"). Somewhere between a flavorful stew and a thick soup, Louisiana gumbo can be made with anything from seasonal Gulf seafood (plump oysters, partially shelled crabs, or peeled shrimp) to wild duck and Cajun sausage. The ingredients for this version are pretty much universal and economical, and they offer a good introduction to this delicious gameday treat.

THE INGREDIENTS

1 cup + 2 tablespoons vegetable oil
1 pound andouille, kielbasa, or smoked sausage, cut into chunks or sliced 1/2-inch thick
1 cup all-purpose flour
1 1/2 cups chopped onions
3/4 cup chopped celery
3/4 cup chopped green bell peppers
3 tablespoons Cajun seasoning (or combine 1 tablespoon freshly ground black pepper, 2 teaspoons salt, and 1 1/2 teaspoons ground red pepper)
6 cups water
3 bay leaves
1 (3 1/2-pound) chicken, cut up, or 6 bone-in chicken breast halves, with or without skin
1/2 cup chopped scallions
6 tablespoons chopped fresh parsley
Cooked white rice

THE DRILL

1. Heat two tablespoons of the oil in a large Dutch oven or cast-iron skillet over medium-high heat. Add the sausages and cook, turning occasionally, until browned. Drain the sausages on paper towels and set aside. Discard the drippings from the Dutch oven.

2. In the same Dutch oven, to make a brown roux, heat the remaining cup of oil over low heat until hot, one to two minutes. Add the flour, 1/4 cup at a time, beating constantly with a whisk or long-handled wooden spoon until each batch is blended. Cook, stirring frequently and taking care to avoid splatters, until the roux gradually changes color — from pasty beige to peanut butter color to chocolate brown — "enough time to drink two beers," 20 to 25 minutes.

3. Add the onions to the roux and cook, stirring frequently, two to three minutes. Add the celery and bell peppers; reduce the heat to low and cook, stirring occasionally, until the vegetables start to soften. Stir in the reserved sausage and one tablespoon of the Cajun seasoning; cook, stirring frequently, until fragrant. Stir in the water and bay leaves until well blended. Rub the remaining two tablespoons of Cajun seasoning all over the chicken. Add the chicken to the pot and bring just to a boil. Reduce the heat and cook at a low simmer, skimming off the fat and stirring occasionally, until the chicken is cooked through and very tender, about 1 1/2 hours. Stir in the scallions and parsley. Remove the bay leaves and serve over rice.

ROOKIE MISTAKE
RUINING THE ROUX

It's been said that every Cajun recipe (and many a Creole soup and sauce) starts with the five-word phrase "first, you make a roux," and with good reason. This foundation gives Cajun dishes their signature richness and deep, nutty flavor. The recipe for roux — equal parts flour and oil — hails from the French kitchen and is the primary thickener and flavoring agent in gumbos, étouffées, and other Louisiana standbys.

Making a roux is like playing stud poker: it takes only a few minutes to learn, but a lifetime to master. The longer you stir the mixture over heat, the darker it gets. The most common types are:

☞ Blonde: A delicate-tasting roux that looks a litttle bit like thin peanut butter, used for darker, more full-flavored meats (especially wild game).

☞ Medium: A versatile beginner's roux that's cooked to the shade of smooth peanut butter. A good match for chicken and sausage gumbos and other mixed-meat dishes.

☞ Chocolate: Could it get more self-explanatory? Aim for a shade lighter than chocolate syrup.

Some cooks swear by an extremely dark roux for their dishes, but the novice should be extremely careful when attempting the darker shades. It doesn't take much to burn the mixture, and once black bits start appearing, it's all over. The culprit is usually impatience and a high flame. When this happens, clean out the pot, pop open another beer, and start again (on low heat this time).

JUMBO JAMBALAYA

SERVES
6

This hearty Cajun classic is the distant cousin of African rice dishes and of the Spanish arroz con pollo (rice cooked with chunks of chicken in a rich broth). Simply, jambalaya is one of the finest, most satisfying autumn and winter dishes out there. The legion of Louisiana tailgaters tend to mix their batches in 20-gallon cast-iron cauldrons and stir them with canoe paddles. Ideally, you'll be able to get hold of a nice, smoky andouille sausage, but a flavorful kielbasa will also do.

HOT LINKS

FRESH OR SMOKED?

Our slow-cooked dishes make liberal use of various species from the sausage food group, so it's probably best to review the different major types.

Fresh These varieties, made from uncooked meats, require a little care. For safety purposes, treat them like raw meat and be aware of the possibility of bacterial cross-contamination (i.e., wash your hands after handling). Treat these as you would ground beef or uncooked poultry:

☞ Breakfast sausage

☞ Country pork sausage

☞ Italian sausage

☞ Chicken/turkey sausage

Cured and Cooked These types are pretty much pre-cooked by the curing and smoking process, so they require a little less caution. But then, would it kill you to wash your hands every once in awhile?

☞ Andouille

☞ Kielbasa

☞ Smoked sausage

THE INGREDIENTS

2 teaspoons olive oil

2 boneless, skinless chicken breast halves, cut into strips

1/2 pound andouille, kielbasa, or smoked sausage, diced

1 medium onion, diced

1 green bell pepper, diced

1/2 cup diced celery

2 tablespoons chopped garlic

1/2 teaspoon onion powder

1/4 teaspoon ground red pepper

Salt and freshly ground pepper, to taste

2 cups white rice

4 cups reduced-sodium chicken broth or homemade chicken stock

3 bay leaves

1 tablespoon Worcestershire sauce

1 teaspoon hot pepper sauce

THE DRILL

1. In a large Dutch oven, heat the oil over medium-high heat. Add the chicken and sausage and cook, stirring occasionally, until lightly browned, about five minutes. Add the onion, bell pepper, celery, garlic, onion powder, red pepper, salt, and ground pepper. Cook, stirring frequently, until the onion is tender, about five minutes. Add the rice, and stir to coat the grains.

2. Stir in the broth and bay leaves, and bring to a boil. Reduce the heat and simmer, covered, until the rice is fully cooked and most of the liquid has evaporated, about 20 minutes. Stir in the Worcestershire and hot pepper sauces.

SERVES 4 TO 6

RAGIN' CAJUN SHRIMP ÉTOUFFÉE

Fans of the University of Louisiana Ragin' Cajuns are partial to this classic dish when shrimp is in season or when crawfish tails (another local delicacy) are in short supply. It's best to work quickly with this recipe, though; a short cooking time will ensure that the precious shrimp won't cook to a rubbery texture.

THE INGREDIENTS

3/4 cup butter
4 cups chopped onions
2 cups chopped green bell peppers
2 cups chopped celery
2 teaspoons chopped garlic
2 pounds medium shrimp, peeled and deveined
I teaspoon salt
I/2 teaspoon ground red pepper
2 cups water
2 tablespoons all-purpose flour
I/2 cup chopped fresh parsley
I/2 cup chopped scallions

THE DRILL

I. In a large skillet, melt the butter over medium heat. Add the onions, bell peppers, and celery; cook, stirring occasionally, until softened and golden, about 10 minutes. Add the garlic and cook, stirring frequently, about two minutes. Add the shrimp, salt, and red pepper; cook, stirring frequently, just until the shrimp turn pink, about four minutes.

2. Meanwhile, in a small bowl, combine the water and flour, beating with a whisk until the flour dissolves. Stir the dissolved flour mixture into the shrimp mixture and cook, stirring occasionally, until the mixture thickens slightly. Reduce the heat and simmer, stirring occasionally, just until the shrimp turn opaque in the center, six to eight minutes. Stir in the parsley and scallions; cook about one minute longer. Serve at once.

CHAPTER 7
HOT PROSPECTS

CASSEROLES AND CHEESY STUFF

CHALK TALK

Do *not* freak out at the sight of the word "casserole" in the section title. Before visions of bored housewives in frilly aprons trying to be "creative" with their leftovers leap into your mind, let's get a few things straight:

I. There are no recipes for "Tuna Noodle Surprise" or "Turkey Tetrazzini" in this section.

2. Under *no* circumstances will you be required to open a can of Cream of Mushroom soup.

3. Take deep breaths and focus on the promise of the "cheesy stuff."

With that said, let us casse-roll ...

Casseroles might be considered a hallmark of bland Midwestern cooking (a comforting, if not exactly complimentary, designation). But when it comes to tailgating, they have plenty going for them. They can be baked at home, hold their heat well, and can be served in disposable aluminum pans. With a bit of fuss on the front end, they cause very little muss at any outdoor gathering. And even the cleanup's a breeze.

Tailgaters in cold-weather climes would do well to embrace the casserole, since these versatile hot dishes can give any party a break from six straight Saturdays of brats and burgers.

Sounds painless, doesn't it?

And as we all know, any worthwhile tailgate has to include a few pounds of a cheese-type substance — be it in the form of savory quesadillas, tangy pimento cheese sandwiches, or an oozy dip. Farmers of Wisconsin (and by extension, all you Badger fans), we salute you.

**SERVES
10 TO 12**

TOUCHBACK BAKED BEANS

Ahhhhhh ... Boston beans by way of suburban Houston. (Thanks, Martha). Whether they're considered a side dish or a supper unto themselves, these savory beans pack enough punch to satisfy Rice fans while paying a pork-spiked homage to the Ivy League.

THE INGREDIENTS

3 (32-ounce) cans pork and beans, drained

2 (16-ounce) tubes fresh country-style pork sausage, cooked
 according to package directions and crumbled

2 medium onions, sliced

1 cup firmly packed brown sugar

1 cup dark corn syrup

1/4 cup yellow mustard

1 tablespoon mustard powder

2 teaspoons Worcestershire sauce

THE DRILL

1. Preheat the oven to 350°F.

2. Combine the pork and beans, cooked sausage, and onions in a 13 x 9-inch baking dish; stir to mix. Add the brown sugar, corn syrup, yellow mustard, mustard powder, and Worcestershire sauce; stir until blended. Bake until bubbly and the beans have thickened slightly, about 1 1/2 hours.

EXTRA POINT

For even better flavor, prepare the recipe in advance. Cool, then cover and refrigerate overnight. Reheat at 350°F for about 30 minutes.

HARD-HITTING MAC AND CHEESE

SERVES 10 TO 12

Sure, we all have a weakness for the powdered cheese version of the boxed mac and cheeses from our youth. But this here recipe is the real deal — the stuff that cheese dreams are made of. It's a bit more complicated to make (it uses *actual* cheese, for example), but the result pays off huge in terms of flavor and satisfaction. Serve in a heavy casserole dish, or, for a twist that turns it into hand-food, let it cool and cut it into squares after the pasta has firmly set.

THE INGREDIENTS

1 (1-pound) box elbow macaroni
1 tablespoon vegetable oil
1/2 cup + 1 tablespoon butter
1/2 cup shredded Muenster cheese
1/2 cup shredded mild cheddar cheese
1/2 cup shredded sharp cheddar cheese
1/2 cup shredded Monterey Jack cheese
1 (1-pint) container half-and-half
1/2 pound Velveeta, cut into small cubes
2 large eggs, lightly beaten
1/4 teaspoon seasoned salt
1/8 teaspoon freshly ground black pepper

PLAYMAKER

HAIL TO THE CHEESE FOOD

Over the years, there's been a distinct shift away from the traditional all-American tailgating aesthetic — basically, from a late-season adaptation of the classic Fourth of July picnic to a more elaborate, gourmet-type presentation. Where once Cheez Whiz preparations abounded, folks are now passing over even American and Swiss for the fancier Gouda and Camembert.

And while that may make sense on some level (ain't nothin' like a slab of extra-sharp white cheddar cheese, my friends), tailgates should be exempt from this kind of "real food" purism. The eternal rules of the tailgate require the bending of most nutritional guidelines to embrace the creamy goodness of cheese food. And besides, any seasoned tailgate cook will tell you that they use Velveeta because "it just melts right."

Consider it a tip of the hat to the food technology of the 1950s, a time when dairy products and plastic polymer technology began to seriously overlap.

If you're still feeling dicey about indulging in bite after bite of smooth, cheese-foody goodness, just spend Monday munching on a kilo of kale or a head of cauliflower to ease your troubled mind.

THE DRILL

1. Preheat the oven to 350°F. Grease a deep 2 1/2-quart baking dish.

2. Bring a large pot of salted water to a boil. Add the macaroni and oil; cook just until tender, about seven minutes. Do not overcook. Drain well. Return the macaroni to the pot.

3. In a small saucepan, melt 1/2 cup of the butter over medium heat. Stir into the macaroni. In a large bowl, combine the Muenster, both cheddars, and Monterey Jack; stir 1 1/2 cups of the shredded cheeses into the macaroni. Stir in the half-and-half, Velveeta, eggs, seasoned salt, and black pepper; spoon into the baking dish. Sprinkle the top with the remaining shredded cheeses and dot with the remaining tablespoon of butter. Bake until it's bubbly around the edges, about 35 minutes.

SEC PIMENTO CHEESE

SERVES 4

In certain parts of the South, this tangy, creamy treat inspires deep loyalties and matching rivalries. For many folks, it's a direct link to their grandmother's kitchen, family tailgates, and fond memories associated with both. Smear this spicy (and yes, bright freakin' orange) spread on doughy white bread or scoop it up with crackers. South Carolina fans will no doubt spoon a thick dollop on top of their burgers in homage to Columbia's Rockaway Athletic Club.

THE INGREDIENTS

1/2 pound extra-sharp or sharp yellow cheddar cheese, shredded

1 (8-ounce) package shredded Velveeta

1/2 to 1 cup Miracle Whip dressing

1 (2-ounce) jar chopped pimentos, drained

2 to 3 teaspoons prepared horseradish, drained

1 teaspoon Worcestershire sauce

1/4 teaspoon onion powder

Freshly ground black pepper

8 slices white bread

THE DRILL

1. To make the filling, in a large bowl, combine the cheddar and Velveeta. Add 1/2 cup of the dressing, stirring with a fork, adding the remaining 1/2 cup of dressing, if necessary, until creamy. Stir in the pimentos, horseradish, Worcestershire sauce, onion powder, and pepper. Transfer the mixture to an airtight container and refrigerate at least overnight or up to a week.

2. Divide the filling between four slices of the bread; top with the remaining bread.

SERVES 8 TO 10

CROWD-PLEASING HOT CHEESE DIP

If there is a universal tailgate food, it is a bowlful of lava-like yellow cheese that earns the honor. This gooey bowl full of boisterous flavor unites one and all—young and old, home and visitor, carnivore and vegetarian—with its combination of creaminess and custom-tailored spice. For most recipes, all you need is a chunk of Velveeta, a can of Ro*Tel tomatoes, a microwave oven, and maybe even a dream. The secret play? Add a little bit of cream cheese into the mix and your dip will stand head and shoulders above the garden-variety two-ingredient version. And as always, pack *plenty* of tortilla chips.

THE INGREDIENTS

1/2 pound Velveeta, cut into cubes
1 (8-ounce) package cream cheese, cut into cubes
1 (10-ounce) can Ro*Tel Original Diced Tomatoes &
    Green Chilies, drained with liquid reserved
Tortilla chips

THE DRILL

Put the Velveeta and cream cheese in a two-quart microwavable bowl. Microwave on high until the cheeses are melted, about four minutes, stirring once halfway through. Stir in the tomatoes and chilies; microwave one minute. Taste. If you want additional heat add some of the reserved tomato liquid, and microwave again. (Can be made ahead of time. Cover and refrigerate up to two days. Know that every time you reheat the dip, it will get spicier.) Serve with tortilla chips.

BEEFED-UP CHILI CON QUESO

MAKES
4 CUPS

Here we have a meaty version of the **Crowd-Pleasing Hot Cheese Dip (p. 143)**—basically the love child of cheese dip and chili con carne. In terms of preparation, think of it as a gameday twin-killing: cook a batch of your favorite chili and of the gooey cheese dip, then create a third dish by simply spooning some of each into a bowl and stirring to combine. Make your own meaty version of concession-stand nachos by spooning a heapin' helpin' on top of tortilla chips, with pickled jalapeños as a garnish.

THE INGREDIENTS

1 (1-pound) package Velveeta, cut into 1-inch chunks
1 cup of homemade chili (such as **Lone Star Chili, p. 111,** or **Fred's Famous Tar Heel Chili, p. 112)** or 1 (15-ounce) can chili without beans
1 (10-ounce) can Ro*Tel Original Diced Tomatoes & Green Chilies, drained
2 chipotle peppers in adobo sauce, chopped ✚ 1 tablespoon adobo sauce
2 tablespoons chopped fresh cilantro
Tortilla chips

THE DRILL

1. Microwave the Velveeta in a two-quart microwavable bowl on high two minutes; stir until smooth. Add the chili, tomatoes and chilies, chipotles, and adobo sauce; stir to combine. Microwave until hot, about two minutes longer.

2. Stir in the cilantro and serve at once with tortilla chips.

VEGETARIAN QUESADILLAS

This south-of-the-border flat bread sandwich, the Southwestern equivalent of your mom's grilled cheese, is a tried-and-true option if you've got vegetarians on your "drop-by" list. The chip-friendly bowl of salsa lets your guests adjust their own heat levels, while a little cup of cooling sour cream can score you a few extra points.

THE INGREDIENTS

1 tablespoon vegetable oil
1 medium onion, sliced
1 medium green bell pepper, sliced
12 (10-inch) flour tortillas
1 1/2 cups shredded Mexican cheese blend
3 scallions, chopped
Salsa, for dipping

THE DRILL

1. In a large skillet, heat the oil over medium-high heat. Add the onion and bell pepper; cook, stirring occasionally, until softened, seven to eight minutes. Transfer the vegetables to a plate and cool slightly. Using tongs, wipe the skillet with a paper towel.

2. Arrange the tortillas on a flat surface. Cover half of each tortilla with some of the vegetables, cheese, and scallions. Fold each tortilla over to cover the filling.

3. Spray the same skillet with nonstick cooking oil and set over medium heat. Add two of the quesadillas and cook until lightly browned, two to three minutes on each side. Transfer the quesadillas to a cutting board and keep warm. Repeat with the remaining quesadillas.

4. Cut each quesadilla into three wedges and serve at once with salsa.

HASH MARK HASH BROWN CASSEROLE

SERVES 8 TO 10

Well, okay. We had to have at least one cream-of-something soup recipe, and here it is. Cheesy, crunchy, and silky all at once, this one is perfect for fans of home fries — especially anyone who craves the taste of a buttery cornflake crust.

THE INGREDIENTS

5 tablespoons butter
1 (8-ounce) package shredded cheddar cheese
1 (10 3/4-ounce) can condensed cream of chicken soup
1 (8-ounce) container sour cream
1/2 cup finely chopped onion
1/2 cup finely chopped green bell pepper
1/2 cup finely chopped red bell pepper
1/4 teaspoon salt
1/4 teaspoon freshly ground black pepper
1 (30- to 32-ounce) package frozen hash browns, thawed
1 cup crushed cornflakes

THE DRILL

1. Preheat the oven to 350°F. Grease a 13 x 9-inch baking dish.

2. Melt four tablespoons of the butter and transfer to a large bowl. Add the cheese, soup, sour cream, onion, bell peppers, salt, and ground pepper; mix well. With a rubber spatula, fold in the hash browns. Spread the mixture in the baking dish.

3. Melt the remaining tablespoon of butter; combine in a small bowl with the cornflakes and sprinkle over the potato mixture. Bake until golden brown and the potatoes are tender, about one hour.

SERVES 10

KICKOFF BREAKFAST CASSEROLE

A crossover dish from our Get Your Game Face On chapter, this versatile and substantial dish is essentially a savory bread pudding topped with a layer of cheese and nuggets of crispy sausage. Horseradish and mustard powder give it just the right amount of flavorful boost. This is the perfect dish for a morning tailgate; just assemble and refrigerate on Friday night and bake it off when you get up on gameday morning.

THE INGREDIENTS

9 large eggs
3 cups whole milk
3/4 teaspoon prepared horseradish
3/4 teaspoon mustard powder
4 cups French bread, cubed
1 pound pork sausage, cooked and crumbled
1 cup shredded cheddar cheese

THE DRILL

1. In a large bowl, combine the eggs, milk, horseradish, and mustard powder, beating with a whisk until blended.

2. Spray a 13 x 9-inch baking dish with nonstick cooking spray; add the bread cubes and spread evenly. Sprinkle the top with the sausage. Pour the egg mixture over the bread and sausage; sprinkle the top with the cheese. Cover the dish with plastic wrap and refrigerate overnight.

3. Preheat the oven to 350°F. Uncover the dish and bake until golden and the center is set, about 45 minutes. Let stand 10 minutes before serving.

STACKED ENCHILADAS

SERVES 8

Essentially a border version of cheese lasagna, this low-maintenance Mexican-style treat doesn't require much cooking finesse to execute, which increases even a novice cook's chance of success with the recipe. The process feels a lot more like dealing out a hand of poker than rolling a pack of cigarettes. The only part that requires a bit of care is the tortilla-frying portion of the program. Cook at your own leisure, work a couple of tortillas at a time, and use your tongs to avoid splashing the oil. And for heaven's sake, make sure you know where your fire extinguisher is. (Not saying anything *will* happen, it's just better to be safe, y'know?)

THE INGREDIENTS

Corn oil, for frying
12 corn tortillas
2 (10 1/2-ounce) cans red or green enchilada sauce
4 cups cooked shredded chicken
2 (8-ounce) packages shredded Monterey Jack cheese
1 cup chopped onion
Sour cream

THE DRILL

1. Preheat the oven to 350°F. Spray a 13 x 9-inch baking dish with non-stick cooking spray. Line a large baking sheet with paper towels. Fill a medium skillet with enough oil to reach 1/4 inch deep. Set the skillet over medium heat and heat until small bubbles appear when a wooden spoon is placed in the oil, about five minutes.

2. Add one tortilla and cook, turning once, until softened, about one minute. Transfer to the paper towels to drain. Repeat with the remaining tortillas. Transfer the tortillas to a cutting board and cut each into quarters.

3. Spread about 1/2 cup of the sauce over the bottom of the baking dish. Layer the top with one-third of the tortillas, 1 1/3 cups of the chicken, 1/3 cup of the onion, 1 1/3 cups of the cheese, and one-third of the remaining sauce. Repeat twice more with the remaining tortillas, chicken, onion, cheese, and sauce. Bake until hot and bubbly, 25 to 35 minutes. Serve hot or at room temperature with sour cream.

SERVES 6 TO 8

NO-HASSLE BAKED ZITI

Of course, you *could* whip up a batch of your Zia Angelina's special lasagna for a tailgate, but why bother with a dish that requires a decent amount of manual dexterity and noodle-wrangling ability? Better go with this toss-and-bake classic that won't leave second-degree pasta burns all over your hands. You'll need them to root with.

THE INGREDIENTS

1 (1-pound) box ziti

1 pound Italian sausage links, casings removed and crumbled

1 cup chopped onion

3 garlic cloves, minced

6 cups prepared marinara sauce or **In the Red Zone Sauce (p. 126)**

1 (8-ounce) package shredded mozzarella cheese

1 cup freshly grated Parmesan cheese

THE DRILL

1. Preheat the oven to 375°F. Grease a 13 x 9-inch baking dish.

2. Cook the ziti to according to package directions. Drain, reserving one cup of the pasta cooking liquid. Set both aside.

3. Set a large skillet over medium-high heat. Add the sausage, onion, and garlic; cook, stirring occasionally, until the onion is softened and the sausage is browned and cooked through, about 10 minutes. Stir in five cups of the sauce and the reserved pasta cooking liquid; bring to a simmer. Cook until the flavors are blended, about 10 minutes. Add the ziti, stirring until well mixed.

4. Spoon half of the ziti mixture into the baking dish; spread evenly. Sprinkle the top with the mozzarella and 1/2 cup of the Parmesan. Layer the top with the remaining ziti mixture, one cup of sauce, and the rest of the Parmesan. Bake until heated through, about 30 minutes. Let stand five minutes before serving or serve at room temperature.

FAKE-OUT BARBECUE SHRIMP

SERVES 10 TO 12

This peel-and-eat New Orleans classic is "barbecue" in name only; it's a simple, oven-baked dish that's all about the sauce. Garlic, rosemary, and black pepper infuse the rich butter sauce, which is soaked up with good French bread. Hosts might want to bring along an extra roll of paper towels for hand-wiping and makeshift bibs for enthusiastic eaters.

THE INGREDIENTS

1 pound butter
1 medium onion, minced
3 celery stalks, minced
8 garlic cloves, minced
3 to 4 tablespoons chopped fresh parsley
2 tablespoons Creole seasoning
2 teaspoons freshly ground black pepper
2 tablespoons fresh rosemary, chopped
3/4 cup good-quality beer
1/2 cup Worcestershire sauce
2 teaspoons fresh lemon juice
5 pounds large shrimp in shells (with heads) or 3 pounds (without heads)
French bread, sliced

THE DRILL

1. Preheat the oven to 350°F. In a medium-size skillet, melt 1/2 cup of the butter over medium-high heat. Add the onion, celery, garlic, parsley, Creole seasoning, black pepper, and rosemary. Cook, stirring frequently, until the vegetables are softened, two to three minutes.

2. In a large saucepan, melt the remaining 1 1/2 cups of butter over medium heat. Remove the pan from the heat and stir in the beer. Stir in the vegetable mixture, Worcestershire sauce, and lemon juice.

3. Spread the shrimp evenly in a 13 x 9-inch baking dish. Pour the butter mixture over the shrimp and toss to coat. Bake until the shrimp are just opaque in the center, about 15 minutes. Serve in big bowls with French bread to soak up sauce.

CHAPTER 8

IT ISN'T EASY BEING GREEN

VEGETABLES AND SALADS

CHALK TALK

When it comes to the traditional football foods, seared meat reigns supreme and gooey cheesy products come in a close second, but vegetables? Unless you invited your mom to whip up a batch of her Peanut Butter Broccoli Surprise, vegetables and salads are probably way down on the priority list for the average tailgate.

But the sad reality is that there will always be someone (your mom, a guest, that cute girl from the marketing division that you've been checking out) who will want to see some kind of vegetable matter on the table. The green salad — tender lettuces dressed in bottled dressing — is the reflex choice, but as any picnic planner will tell your, crisp greens don't last long out-of-doors. They wilt, flatten out, and puddle up pretty quickly.

Our collection of vegetable dishes puts a premium on durability. Our greens are made of hearty cabbages and iceberg lettuces that keep their crunch for hours on the buffet table. Same goes for the salads and picnic time favorites. (Have you ever tried to have real barbecue without potato salad? Well, this is no time to start.)

TIMEOUT SMOTHERED CABBAGE

SERVES 6 TO 8

This is a New Year's favorite, a great way to get your helping of good-luck greens before the bowl game clock runs out. Most people boil this versatile green Irish-style — but if you slow-cook it with caramelized onions, tangy **Top-Ranked Olive Salad**, and crispy smoked sausage, you'll find your guests going back for extra luck.

THE INGREDIENTS

3 tablespoons vegetable or olive oil

1/2 pound baked ham, diced, or smoked sausage, sliced 1/8-inch thick

2 medium onions, diced

I (28-ounce) can whole tomatoes in puree (chopped or smashed between your fingers)

1/2 to 3/4 cup amber beer (nothing *too* dark here)

1/2 cup **Top-Ranked Olive Salad (p. 157)** or pitted green olives, finely chopped

I teaspoon dried basil

Salt, freshly ground pepper, and hot pepper sauce, to taste

I (2- to 3-pound) head green cabbage, cored and coarsely chopped

THE DRILL

I. In a large Dutch oven, heat the oil over medium heat. Add the ham or sausage and cook until browned and crisp. Add the onions in two batches and cook, stirring occasionally, until the onions are lightly browned. Stir in the tomatoes, beer, olive salad, olives, and basil; increase the heat and bring just to a simmer.

2. Add the cabbage in batches and cook, stirring frequently, until the leaves wilt after each addition. (Don't worry; huge mounds of cabbage lose their bulk pretty quickly when cooked.) Reduce the heat and simmer, covered, until the cabbage is tender, about 45 minutes. Stir in the salt, ground pepper, and hot pepper sauce.

OLE MISS SEVEN-LAYER SALAD

SERVES 8

This multilayered salad can be assembled the previous night in your largest bowl and then stored in the fridge until it's time for the game. This staple at Southern picnic tables gets its tang and creaminess from Miracle Whip, a little bacon, and hard-boiled eggs (thrown in for good measure).

THE INGREDIENTS

6 cups shredded iceberg lettuce

2 cups chopped tomatoes

2 cups sliced fresh mushrooms

1 (10-ounce) package frozen peas, thawed and drained

1 cup shredded cheddar cheese ✚ extra for garnish (optional)

1 cup red onion, sliced into rings

2 cups Miracle Whip dressing

3 large eggs, hard-boiled, peeled, and chopped

2 slices bacon, cooked until crisp and chopped

THE DRILL

1. In a two-quart serving bowl, layer five cups of the lettuce, the tomatoes, mushrooms, peas, cheese, and red onion. Top with the dressing, spreading to the edge of the bowl to form a seal. Sprinkle the remaining cup of lettuce over the top. Cover the bowl with plastic wrap and refrigerate until thoroughly chilled, at least two hours or overnight.

2. To serve, uncover the salad and sprinkle the top with the bacon, egg, and additional cheese (if using).

CLASSIC TAIL-GATING

OXFORD, MISSISSIPPI

For Ole Miss fans, football is a formal affair. They strut about the illustrious Grove beneath red, white, and blue tents in their Sunday best: coats and ties for the gentlemen, Oscar-worthy eveningwear for the ladies. You'll never find a more picturesque setting for a tailgate. But think champagne glasses, fine china, and chandeliers, not charcoal grills and paper plates. The university has strict rules against anything that might mar the landscape.

BILL CURRY SAYS, "The Grove has more candelabra, turnip greens, biscuits, and red-eye gravy per capita than the Delta. And they really do redshirt Miss Americas."

IMPOSSIBLE-TO-MUFF MUFFULETTA

SERVES 12

A big dollop of **Top-Ranked Olive Salad** is required to make this rendition of a classic New Orleans specialty — essentially an antipasto platter on seeded bread. In the Crescent City, sandwich joints and grocery stores use round loaves of coarse-crumbed Italian bread about 10 inches in diameter topped with tasty layers of hearty, delicatessen-style meats and cheeses: fragrant hard salami, Swiss and provolone cheeses, smooth-textured mortadella (Italian bologna), and paper-thin shavings of spicy Italian ham. If you can't find a proper muffuletta loaf, then substitute a lightly toasted Italian bread.

THE INGREDIENTS

2 large French *boules* or round crusty Italian breads,
    preferably with sesame seeds, split
2 cups **Top-Ranked Olive Salad (opposite)**
1/2 pound thinly sliced mortadella
1/2 pound thinly sliced boiled ham
1/2 pound thinly sliced Genoa salami
1/2 pound thinly sliced prosciutto
1/2 pound thinly sliced mozzarella cheese
1/2 pound thinly sliced provolone cheese

THE DRILL

1. Place the bottom halves of the bread, cut side up, on a work surface. Spoon 1/2 cup of the olive salad on top of each. Layer each with half of the mortadella, ham, salami, prosciutto, mozzarella, provolone, and remaining olive salad. Cover with the remaining bread.

2. Press down on the top of each sandwich to allow the juices from the olive salad to soak into the bread and filling. Cut each sandwich into six wedges. (If preparing ahead of time, do not cut into wedges. Tightly wrap in plastic and refrigerate up to six hours.)

MAKES
ABOUT
3 CUPS

TOP-RANKED OLIVE SALAD

Think of this as an antipasto platter you can smear on a sandwich. This New Orleans coarse-textured cousin of French tapenade brings together the bright flavors of pickled vegetables with the salty richness of good olives and the punch of raw garlic. It's integral to the **Impossible-to-Muff Muffuletta (opposite)** and **Timeout Smothered Cabbage (p. 154)**.

THE INGREDIENTS

1 (11.1-ounce) jar pitted kalamata olives in brine, drained
1 (16-ounce) jar Greek giardiniera
1 (8-ounce) jar cocktail onions in vinegar, drained
1 (6-ounce) jar pimento-stuffed green olives, drained
1/4 cup olive oil
2 to 3 garlic cloves
1 tablespoon dried oregano
1 celery stalk, chopped

THE DRILL

1. Put all the ingredients except the celery in a food processor. Pulse three to four times until chopped.

2. Add the celery and pulse two times just until blended. Transfer to a bowl; serve at once or refrigerate in an airtight container for up to three weeks.

ROOKIE MISTAKE

A LITTLE TEMP WORK

Most of us don't think much about salads once we put them out on the tailgate table. After all, they're mostly served at room temperature, right? Well, when you're standing outside in Austin, Texas, Gainesville, Florida, or elsewhere in the Sun Belt (region, not conference), you've got no real control over the climate, and therefore very little control over the temperature of your foodstuffs. Once cold food starts getting hot, things can get bacterially funky right quick.

If you're in charge of the buffet table, sample your cold veggies every once in a while to make sure they're still in the lower end of the temperature spectrum. If they're getting too warm, set them on ice in a food cooler for a few minutes, just to knock them down a few degrees.

AGAINST-THE-GRAIN CHICKEN SALAD

SERVES 4 TO 6

Most chicken salad recipes aim for a pleasant, creamy texture—and flavor that's about as interesting as straight mayonnaise. This simple variation substitutes two other condiment-shelf favorites—bottled barbecue sauce and tangy, whole-grain mustard—for the creamy stuff. Finely minced red onion adds bite and a bit of crunch to the final product. Slather onto French bread for a kickin' Monday morning lunch. It's a great way to use up any cooked chicken left over from game day.

THE INGREDIENTS

I pound cooked boneless, skinless chicken breasts; roasted, poached, or grilled, and shredded
I/2 cup whole-grain mustard
I/4 cup favorite barbecue sauce
I small red onion, finely chopped

THE DRILL

Place the chicken in a large bowl. In a small bowl, combine the mustard and barbecue sauce; fold mustard mixture into the chicken until blended. Stir in the red onion.

EXTRA POINT

To mellow the flavor of the red onion, first rinse it in a sieve under cold water. Drain well before adding to the chicken salad.

**SERVES
6 TO 8**

BULLDOG NOODLE SALAD

Ramen noodles—that dorm-room, hot-plate favorite—return in this simple salad that's all about crunch. (Hell, it's got more nuts and noodles than it does greens.) Dry ramen is used commonly in Georgia, so Bulldog fans ought to know better than to cook the noodles before tossing them into the bowl.

THE INGREDIENTS

I/2 cup sugar
I/3 cup white vinegar
I cup vegetable oil
2 (3-ounce) packages chicken-flavored ramen noodles,
    uncooked, and flavor packets
I (16-ounce) package coleslaw mix
I cup slivered almonds, toasted
3/4 cup chopped scallions
I/2 cup sunflower seeds
2 teaspoons sesame seeds, toasted

THE DRILL

I. In a medium bowl, combine the sugar and vinegar, beating with a whisk until the sugar is dissolved. Whisk in the oil and the flavor packets from the noodles. Set the dressing and noodles aside.

2. In a large bowl, combine the coleslaw mix, almonds, scallions, sunflower seeds, and sesame seeds. Break up the noodles into small pieces and stir into the coleslaw mixture. Just before serving, drizzle the salad with the dressing and toss to coat.

KICKBACK COLESLAW

SERVES ABOUT 12

The sweet, pasty coleslaw that they pump out at fast-food chicken joints doesn't hold a candle to this tangy version. Horseradish gives every forkful an added *whump* of tastiness, making it a great match for barbecue and other bold flavors.

THE INGREDIENTS

1 1/4 cups water
1/3 cup apple-cider vinegar
2 1/2 tablespoons sugar
2 (16-ounce) packages coleslaw mix

For the dressing:
3/4 cup mayonnaise
1 tablespoon white vinegar
2 1/2 tablespoons sugar
2 1/2 teaspoons prepared horseradish
2 teaspoons sour cream
1/8 teaspoon paprika

THE DRILL

1. In a large bowl, combine the water, cider vinegar, and sugar, stirring until the sugar is dissolved. Add the coleslaw mix and toss well. Marinate in the refrigerator at least one hour and up to two. Drain thoroughly.

2. To make the dressing, in a small bowl, combine all the ingredients.

3. Add 1/2 cup of the dressing to the drained coleslaw mix and stir well. Add the remaining dressing, 1/4 cup at a time, until the slaw reaches desired consistency.

EXTRA POINT

Refrigerate any remaining dressing in an airtight container up to a week. It makes a good spread for a roast beef sandwich.

SERVES 20

PLAY-ACTION PESTO PASTA SALAD

You gotta love this — corkscrew pasta cleverly disguised as a green thanks to the magical camouflaging properties of pesto. This version does an economical double-fake with flat-leaf parsley standing in for the traditional basil and toasted walnuts subbing for pine nuts. It also goes particularly well with grilled chicken breasts, and any leftover chicken can be cut into chunks for an "eat at work" take-a-long lunch for your girlfriend. You are *so* thoughtful ...

THE INGREDIENTS

1 large bunch flat-leaf parsley, stems removed
1/2 cup good-quality olive oil
6 large garlic cloves, peeled
Salt and freshly ground black pepper, to taste
1 1/4 cups walnuts, toasted
2 (1-pound) boxes fusilli (corkscrew) pasta
5 large, ripe tomatoes, diced
3/4 pound feta cheese, crumbled
3 carrots, cut into matchstick-thin strips
2 green bell peppers, finely chopped
Juice of 3 lemons

THE DRILL

1. To make the pesto, finely chop the parsley in a food processor. With the machine running, gradually add the oil and garlic through the feed tube until blended. Add the salt and pepper; pulse to blend. Add 1/4 cup of the toasted walnuts and pulse four times, until just blended. Transfer to a large bowl and set aside.

2. Cook the fusilli according to package directions. Drain and rinse the fusilli under cold water until cool. Drain well.

3. Add the fusilli to the pesto; toss well to coat. Stir in the remaining ingredients and additional salt and pepper, if necessary. Serve at once or refrigerate until chilled.

ALL-CONFERENCE POTATO SALAD

SERVES 8

A trusty utility player. Not some tarted-up version with roasted potatoes and blanched French green beans, and no herb-infused vinaigrette. This is a potato salad that performs well at any backyard barbecue, tailgate, or Fourth of July picnic. As always, keep it chilled until just about mealtime — both for flavor and safety's sake. (Bayou State bonus points: hardcore traditionalists in Louisiana like to serve their gumbo with scoop of potato salad on the side, balancing hot and hearty with cool and creamy in alternating bites.)

THE INGREDIENTS

2 1/2 pounds russet potatoes, peeled and cut into chunks
2 teaspoons kosher salt
1 (16-ounce) jar sweet gherkins, drained and chopped with juice reserved
1 cup chopped sweet onion (such as Vidalia)
3 large eggs, hard-boiled, peeled, and coarsely chopped
1 cup Miracle Whip dressing
1/4 cup sugar, or to taste
2 teaspoons white vinegar, or to taste
1/2 teaspoon yellow mustard

THE DRILL

1. In a large Dutch oven, combine the potatoes, salt, and enough water to cover. Cover and bring to a boil over medium-high heat. Reduce the heat, uncover, and simmer the potatoes until very soft when tested with a fork. Drain and transfer to a large bowl. With a potato masher or hand-held mixer, beat the potatoes until smooth. Stir in the gherkins, sweet onion, and eggs.

2. In a small bowl, combine the Miracle Whip, sugar, vinegar, and mustard, beating with a whisk until blended. Add the dressing mixture to the warm potato mixture; stir to combine. Serve warm or at room temperature.

CHAPTER 9 ☞
THE SUGAR BOWL

SWEETS AND DESSERTS

CHALK TALK

Even though most tailgates tend to be family affairs, odds are your mama ain't gonna show up at yours to throw down the "no dessert before you finish your dinner" rule. (Which is a highly overrated regulation, especially during football season.) We say you should eat your sweets whenever you damn well please. Heck, they're all out on the table for your impulse-dining pleasure in the first place.

One of the great joys of any tailgate is the "graze as you go" aesthetic. Load up your plate with **Jayhawk Double-Clutch Pork Ribs (p. 97)** and **Drunken Pumpkin Pie (p. 166)**, and keep on alternating between the sweet and the salty. Whatever lights up your taste buds.

The enticing confections collected here cover a solid swath of sugary food groups, with entries from the candy, cake, cheesecake, pie, and pudding categories. Whether you're munching between burgers or waiting until meal's end, your mother probably won't hold it against you too badly on gameday.

DRUNKEN PUMPKIN PIE

SERVES 8

Here's one from the Ivy League. Dartmouth alum and Oklahoma native David Hogsett came up with this riff on Thanksgiving's favorite dessert, topped by a crunchy pecan layer. Make this one the night before for a double bonus: The custard will have time to set, and your house will smell phenomenal.

THE INGREDIENTS

2/3 cup granulated sugar
1 1/2 teaspoons ground cinnamon
1/2 teaspoon salt
1/2 teaspoon ground ginger
1/2 teaspoon ground nutmeg
1/4 teaspoon ground allspice
1/4 teaspoon ground cloves
1 2/3 cups light cream
1 1/2 cups canned solid-pack pumpkin
2 large eggs, beaten
2 tablespoons rum or bourbon whiskey
1 (9-inch) prepared pie shell
1/2 cup firmly packed brown sugar
6 tablespoons butter
1 1/2 cups shelled pecans

THE DRILL

1. Preheat the oven to 425°F. To make the filling, in a large bowl, combine the granulated sugar, cinnamon, salt, ginger, nutmeg, allspice, and cloves. In a medium bowl, combine the cream, pumpkin, eggs, and rum, and beat with a whisk until blended. Add the pumpkin mixture to the sugar mixture, and beat with a whisk until blended.

2. Pour the filling into the pie shell and bake for 15 minutes. Reduce the oven temperature to 350°F and bake another 20 minutes.

3. Meanwhile, to make the topping, in a medium saucepan, combine the brown sugar and butter. Cook over medium heat, stirring occasionally, until the butter is melted and the brown sugar dissolves. Add the pecans and stir to coat.

4. Remove the pie from the oven. Spoon the topping over the filling. Return the pie to the oven and bake until the filling is just set, about 10 minutes longer. Cool completely on a wire rack.

COMMODORE CHESS PIE

SERVES
8

A classic Deep South dessert, this pie transforms many household basics — eggs, sugar, and a splash of vinegar, believe it or not — into a high-octane sweet that's as addictive as it is simple to make. Give a nod to Vanderbilt on this one.

THE INGREDIENTS

1 1/3 cups sugar
1/3 cup butter or margarine, softened
3 large eggs
1/3 cup whole milk
1 tablespoon self-rising cornmeal mix
1 teaspoon vanilla extract
1 teaspoon white vinegar
1 (9-inch) prepared pie shell

THE DRILL

1. Preheat the oven to 350°F. In a medium bowl, beat the sugar and butter with an electric mixer on medium-high speed until the mixture is light and fluffy. Add the eggs, one at a time, beating well after each addition. Beat in the milk, cornmeal mix, vanilla, and vinegar, until just blended. Pour the filling into the pie shell.

2. Bake until a knife inserted one inch from the center comes out clean, about 40 to 45 minutes (the center of the filling will continue to set as the pie cools). Cool on a wire rack for at least one hour. This pie can also be served at room temperature or chilled.

MAKES 24 BARS

SUGAR RUSH CARAMEL-PECAN BARS

Better than a candy bar on any given day, this double-layer dessert marries a sweet, yellow cake base with a gooey, toasted-nut topping. You can bake these a few days ahead, wrap them in wax paper, and store them in a plastic container. But beware temptation: It takes the strongest willpower to avoid sampling them before gameday.

THE INGREDIENTS

For the crust:
1 (18 1/4-ounce) package yellow cake mix
1/2 cup butter, melted
1 large egg

For the filling:
1 (14-ounce) can sweetened condensed milk
1 large egg
1 teaspoons vanilla extract
1 cup chopped pecans, toasted*
1/2 cup toffee bits (such as Heath Bits O' Brickle)

THE DRILL

1. To make the crust, preheat the oven to 350°F. Lightly spray a 13 x 9-inch baking pan with nonstick cooking spray. In a large bowl, beat the cake mix, melted butter, and egg with an electric mixer on high speed until crumbly. Press into the baking pan.

2. To make the filling, in small bowl, combine the condensed milk, egg, and vanilla, and beat with a whisk until blended. Stir in pecans and toffee bits until blended. Spread over the crust in the pan.

3. Bake until a toothpick inserted in the center comes out clean, about 35 minutes. Cool completely on a wire rack. Cut into 24 squares.

---

*To toast the pecans, spread the nuts in a single layer on a baking sheet. Bake at 350°F until fragrant, six to eight minutes. Cool completely.

GAME-WINNING CHEESECAKE

SERVES 12

Consider your cheesecake-making technique an investment, since mastering this complicated baking form offers the fastest way to tailgate fame. This insanely rich dish takes some care to make, but when done right, it always draws a flock of admirers.

THE INGREDIENTS

For the crust:
1 (7-ounce) package Pepperidge Farm Bordeaux Cookies, crushed
2 tablespoons melted butter

For the filling:
4 (8-ounce) packages cream cheese, at room temperature
2 cups sugar
6 large eggs
2 teaspoons vanilla extract
1 (16-ounce) container sour cream

THE DRILL

1. To make the crust, preheat the oven to 375°F. Generously grease the bottom of a nine-inch springform pan (do not grease the sides). In a small bowl, combine the cookie crumbs and melted butter, and mix until the crumbs are evenly moistened. Press into the bottom of the pan. Bake until the edges are lightly browned, 8 to 10 minutes. Cool completely on a wire rack.

2. Meanwhile, to make the filling, in a large bowl, beat the cream cheese with an electric mixer on low speed until creamy. Increase the speed to medium, and gradually beat in the sugar, until light and fluffy. Add the eggs, one at a time, beating well after each addition. Beat in the vanilla. With a rubber spatula, fold in the sour cream.

3. Pour the filling over the crust in the pan. Bake 45 minutes. Turn off the oven and let the cheesecake remain in the oven with the door closed for one hour. Transfer the cheesecake to a wire rack and cool completely. Cover and refrigerate until chilled, at least eight hours, or overnight. To serve, run a sharp knife around the edge of the pan to loosen the cheesecake, and remove the springform ring.

ROOKIE MISTAKE

CUTTING THE CHEESECAKE

Sometimes serving dessert can be tougher than making it in the first place. Bring an uncut cheesecake to a tailgate, and you're just asking for chaos. For one, the rich texture that makes the cake so appealing also makes it a nightmare to cut at warmer temperatures. Those perfect wedges you see in restaurants? They were probably done with the QuesoCutter 3000, an elaborate contraption that combines industrial laser and cryogenic freezing technologies. All kidding aside, slicing a cheesecake should be done with either a long, thin knife or with a length of really strong fishing line. Either method will get the job done, but if you don't feel totally confident about your kitchen skills, go with the "Freshmen" option below. On the bright side, even if you completely screw up the portioning process, tailgaters tend to be very forgiving when it comes to the guy who made the cheesecake.

FRESHMEN If you go with the knife, dip it in hot water to pre-heat the blade (this minimizes the metal sticking to the sweet stuff). Cut all the way through the cake, and pull the blade out horizontally instead of back up through the freshly sliced sweetness. Rewarm the blade with each slice, and you'll have the cheesecake divided up in no time.

UPPERCLASSMEN The fishing line method takes some finesse but makes for a clean, smooth slice once you get the hang of it. Take a four-foot length of stout fishing line and wrap the ends around your hands in a "piano-wire serial killer" kind of grip. Using consistent pressure, press through the cake in a single motion (the line should zip through without sticking), then let go with one hand and pull the line through the cake. Repeat.

UNCLE PABLEAUX'S HAIL MARY CHOCOLATE CHEESECAKE

SERVES 12

This riff on the basic cheesecake is every bit as rich as its more traditional cousin, with the added flavor of chocolate and a hint of orange. That thing we said before about cheesecake fame? Double it for this recipe.

THE INGREDIENTS

For the crust:
11 Oreo cookies, finely crushed
3 tablespoons melted butter

For the filling:
3 (8-ounce) packages cream cheese, at room temperature
3/4 cup sugar
5 teaspoons cornstarch
4 large eggs
1 large egg yolk
1 (12-ounce) bag semisweet chocolate chips, melted
3/4 cup sour cream
Zest of 1 orange, finely grated
1 1/2 teaspoons Mexican vanilla extract
3/4 teaspoon ground cinnamon

For the glaze:
1 (12-ounce) bag semisweet chocolate chips
2 tablespoons vegetable shortening
1/8 teaspoon ground cinnamon

THE DRILL

1. Preheat the oven to 375°F. To make the crust, combine the cookie crumbs and melted butter in a small bowl, and mix until the crumbs are

evenly moistened. Press into the bottom of a nine-inch springform
pan. Bake until the edges are lightly browned, 8 to 10 minutes. Cool
completely on a wire rack.

2. Meanwhile, to make the filling, in a large bowl, beat the cream cheese,
sugar, and cornstarch with an electric mixer on medium speed until
smooth. Add the eggs and egg yolk, one at a time, beating well after each
addition. Beat in the melted chocolate, sour cream, orange zest, vanilla,
and cinnamon.

3. Pour the filling over the crust in the pan. Bake for 45 minutes. Turn
off the oven, and let the cheesecake remain in the oven with the door
closed for one hour. (The cheesecake should jiggle a little in the center.
This means the filling will be nice and creamy. The center will continue
to set as the cake cools.) Transfer the cheesecake to a wire rack and cool
completely. Cover and refrigerate until chilled, at least eight hours,
or overnight.

4. To make the glaze, combine the chocolate chips and shortening in
a microwavable bowl. Microwave on high in 30-second bursts, stirring
between each, until smooth. Run a sharp knife around the edges of the
pan to loosen the cheesecake, and remove the springform ring. Spread the
glaze over the top of the cheesecake, and let stand until the glaze sets.

WILDCAT WHISKEY BREAD PUDDING

SERVES
8

This New Orleans dessert owes a flavorful debt to the whiskey-distilling folk of central Kentucky. Traditionally a good way to make the most of stale bread, bread pudding is a great portable sweet for the tailgate crowd. In this version, the whiskey might sneak up on you — it's cleverly stashed in raisins that have been rehydrated with fine, brown liquor. Tennessee fans will insist on using their home state's sour mash "sipping whiskey," whereas Florida fans might lean toward rum as their spirit of choice.

THE INGREDIENTS

I cup raisins
I/3 cup bourbon whiskey
I tablespoon grated orange zest
I cup sugar
4 large eggs
3 cups whole milk
I teaspoon vanilla extract
7 cups cubed white bread, lightly toasted
Freshly grated nutmeg
I/4 cup butter
Heavy or whipping cream (optional)

THE DRILL

I. In a small bowl, combine the raisins, bourbon, and orange zest, and let stand until the raisins soften, about 20 minutes.

2. Grease a 13 x 9-inch baking dish. In a large bowl, combine the sugar and eggs, and beat with a whisk until blended. Whisk in the milk and vanilla. Combine the bread and raisin mixture in the baking dish, and spread evenly. Pour the egg mixture over the bread mixture and let stand for 15 minutes.

3. Meanwhile, preheat the oven to 375°F. Sprinkle the top of the pudding with nutmeg and dot with butter. Bake on the center oven rack until set and golden brown, about 40 to 45 minutes. Serve warm or at room temperature, drizzled with cream (if using).

MAKES
ABOUT 36
CANDIES

PEANUT BUTTER
BUCKEYES

An insanely easy-to-make candy that looks a lot like the famous nut of Ohio's state tree as well as Ohio State's symbol. The actual buckeye is a form of horse chestnut that, when eaten, might result in all kinds of unthinkable intestinal troubles. It's probably wiser to go for these sweet, bite-size globes with the famous peanut butter/chocolate flavor combo instead.

THE INGREDIENTS

1 (2-pound) bag confectioners' sugar
3 cups creamy peanut butter
3/4 cup butter, softened
1 (7-ounce) tub dipping chocolate, melted according to
    package directions

THE DRILL

1. Line a large tray or baking sheet with wax paper. In a large bowl, combine the confectioners' sugar, peanut butter, and butter, stirring until well blended. Shape into one-inch balls.

2. With a toothpick, dip each ball into the dipping chocolate until almost covered, leaving some of the peanut butter mixture exposed on top. Place the balls on the tray and refrigerate until firm, about two hours.

OHIO STADIUM CAKE

In 1991, a group of devoted Buckeye football fans decided to construct an edible homage to their home turf: a scale model of Ohio Stadium made out of cake, complete with green icing turf, multiple seating decks, and a capacity crowd clad in red and white. Now an annual tradition, the sweet structure (which weighs in at more than 200 pounds) helps fill stadium seats with future fans by raising money for a scholarship fund.

ACKNOWLEDGMENTS

Like so many big projects, *GameDay Gourmet* started out as a bright idea and a tablecloth full of lunchtime scribbles. I'm grateful to the diverse group of friends and professionals who teamed up to put this book in your hands.

First and foremost would be food writer and recipe developer Fred Thompson. As a friend, brother in arms, and enthusiastic tailgate chef, he shaped the book and shared secret recipes from his kitchen lab in North Carolina, his satellite home in Tennessee, and the highways in between. Ms. Belinda Ellis gets a shout-out for keeping him sane during the process.

A couple of tireless editors managed to keep their eyes on all the details even as the clock ticked down to zero. Carol Prager kept track of everything kitchen-related, down to the last 10th of an ounce. Ever calm in the clutch, Bill Vourvoulias pulled off an astounding amount of last-minute heavy lifting.

Thanks to the TV guys: Chris Fowler, Kirk Herbstreit, Lee Corso, Mike Golic, and Bill Curry. They brought the football and the funny.

Chris Raymond headed up the squad at ESPN Books in New York City, from recruiting reporters Scott DeSimon and Brendan O'Connor to calling in assists from Roger Jackson, Chris Lindsley, Lou Monaco, and J.B. Morris. Shauna DeGeorge and Gregory Blanco helped to keep the facts straight. Designers Christina Bliss, Mary Sexton, and Bill Geller and illustrator Christian Sean Rogers made the scribbles look good.

And, of course, additional thanks go to the many friends and fans who contributed their time, effort, and secrets to the time-pressed process. John Currance and John T. Edge acted as sufficiently bad influences in Oxford, Mississippi. Stuart Wade gave a great crash course in NCAA nuance, and Todd Alley is probably still laughing. Sara Roahan gets props for her great timing and fresh set of eyes. Philip Paulsen (the nephew) tolerated his share of stupid questions, and Galen Dixon kicked it all off many years ago with his War Eagle enthusiasm. And we can't forget the LSU contingent: Noel and Jimbo Prescott; the Brothers P (Jimmy, Clint, and Davis); Joey Nolan *y su familia*; Brenda and Charlie Antie (Tigers tailgaters emeritus), and their standard bearer, Brian Antie.

And a special thanks to all the fans who bring the party out to the parking lot. See you round the tables.

Pableaux Johnson
New Orleans
April 2007

INDEX

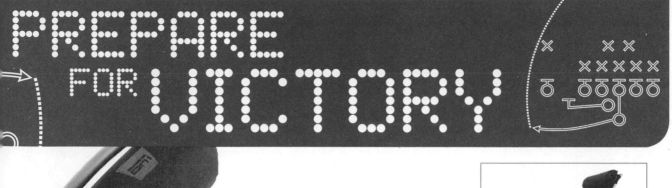

PREPARE FOR VICTORY

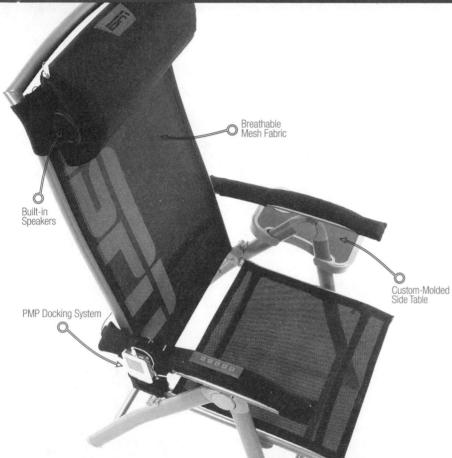

Breathable Mesh Fabric

Built-in Speakers

PMP Docking System

Custom-Molded Side Table

ESPN ULTIMATE TAILGATE COLLECTION

ESPN

 3 KEYS TO VICTORY

○ ESPN MVP LOUNGER
- ⊙ Lightweight aluminum construction
- ⊙ Curvilinear design
- ⊙ Adjustable seating positions
- ⊙ Breathable mesh fabric
- ⊙ Padded arm and headrests
- ⊙ Utility pockets
- ⊙ Speakers
- ⊙ Ability to connect PMPs
- ⊙ Easy setup/takedown

○ ESPN STADIUM PAVILION
- ⊙ New domed pavilion w/interior space
- ⊙ Customized modular table system w/2 cup holders
- ⊙ Utility storage pocket
- ⊙ Mesh wall system
- ⊙ Hooks and fasteners for team affinity
- ⊙ Diagonal extension wall
- ⊙ Easy setup/takedown
- ⊙ Portable
- ⊙ Convenient carrying case

○ ESPN SIDELINE GRILL STATION
- ⊙ Lightweight aluminum construction
- ⊙ Dual side tables
- ⊙ ESPN-branded apron
- ⊙ Utility pocket
- ⊙ Grid shelving system
- ⊙ Portable
- ⊙ Convenient carrying case

ESPN TAILGATING STARTS AT

EVERY SEASON STARTS AT **DICK'S SPORTING GOODS**

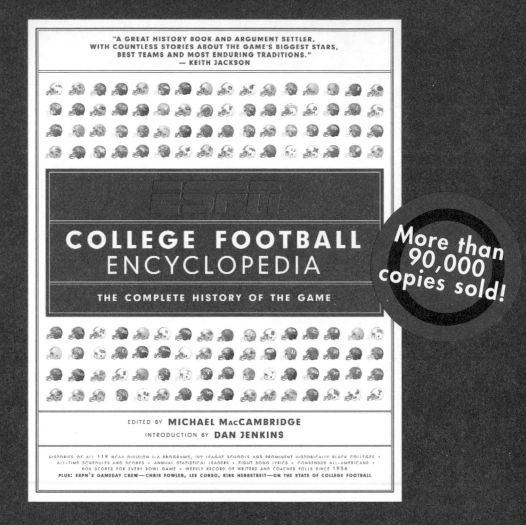